# Strange Meetings

### by Anne Bradford
### & Barrie Roberts

# QuercuS

**\*\*\*\*\*\*\*\*\*\*\*\*\*\*\*\*\*\*\*\*\*\*\*\***

## QuercuS
The Garden House
John Roberts
67, Cliffe Way, Warwick
CV34 5JG   01926 776363
**\*\*\*\*\*\*\*\*\*\*\*\*\*\*\*\*\*\*\*\*\*\*\*\***

## Strange Meetings

by Anne Bradford & Barrie Roberts

ISBN 1 898136 21 1

First Published 2002

# Preface

QuercuS publishes books about the western Midlands, that area between the rivers Trent, Severn and Avon that geographers call the 'Midland Triangle'. We have published books about the history of the area (castles, coaching, historic houses), the countryside (woods and rivers), and murders. More peaceably there are the albums of pen and ink sketches of buildings in HalesOwen, Bromsgrove and Birmingham, and two autobiographies. One of the most popular subjects has been ghosts and the paranormal with two books by Anne Bradford and Barrie Roberts, *Midland Ghosts & Hauntings* and *Midland Spirits & Spectres*. We didn't need any encouragement to bring out this third book.

# The Authors

**ANNE BRADFORD** was a secretary and a school teacher before she turned to writing and publishing. This began in 1992 when a librarian in her home town of Redditch showed her some local Victorian ghost stories and added that he was looking for someone to update them by adding contemporary eye witness accounts. Anne took it on and published her first book, *Haunted*, under her own imprint, Hunt End Books. This was followed by *Haunted Worcestershire* (1996), *Haunted Pubs and Hotels* (1998), and *Unquiet Spirits of Worcestershire* (1999). She has also produced two local history books, *Royal Enfield* (1996) and William Avery's *Old Redditch* (1999). With Barrie Roberts she has written *Midland Ghosts & Hauntings* (1996) and *Midland Spirits and Spectres* (1998), published by QuercuS.

**BARRIE ROBERTS** is a former legal consultant and lectures an evening course on the paranormal for Birmingham City Council. He is an internationally published writer whose works have been translated into Latvian, Indonesian, Russian and even American. He has written six Sherlock Holmes pastiches and a number of modern mystery novels. For QuercuS he wrote with Anne the two collections of ghost stories named above and on his own, *Midland Murders and Mysteries* and *Murder in the Midlands*.

# Contents

## Worcestershire

# Do You
# Believe in Ghosts?

Take any ten scientists and ask them if they believe in ghosts. At least eight of them will assure you that they don't and explain at length why ghosts cannot possibly exist. Of the other two, one will hum and haw (well out of earshot of his colleagues) and eventually say that maybe there are certain aspects of the paranormal that might bear investigation. If you are amazingly lucky, the tenth will tell you that he, or she, would love to investigate ghosts if only someone would pay them to do it.

Now take any ten members of the lay public and put the same question. Many of them will tell you that they, personally, don't actually believe in ghosts, but they will quite likely go on to describe a weird experience of their own or something strange that happened to Aunt Agatha. More than half of your group will tell you that they do believe in ghosts, and almost all of them will be able to tell you about a strange experience of their own or a friend or relative.

You might find this second group surprising if you don't know that ghostly happenings have been recorded since the dawn of history in every part of the populated world, and that the statisticians say the British Isles are the most haunted place in the world. That makes the first group much more surprising.

Like our two previous QuercuS books, *Midland Ghosts & Hauntings* and *Midland Spirits & Spectres*, this book is for both groups. It will assure the second group that they are not crazy, there really is something strange going on, and it will demonstrate to the first group that there is really rather a lot of evidence in favour of the idea they reject, more than a lot, in fact, a mountain of it.

Like the other books this one consists almost entirely of accounts of paranormal experiences by ordinary people all over the western Midlands. Set right at the heart of these deeply haunted islands, this area includes almost every kind of British town and landscape. We have crowded inner cities and industrial estates, pretty villages and sixties tower blocks, wild moorlands and orderly suburbs, stately homes and crumbling slums. Any of them may be haunted.

The hundreds of people who supply us with stories of their experiences are from all walks of life, from various religions and none. In one radio phone-in we heard from someone whose encounter with a ghost had destroyed their religious belief and another whose experience had caused them to start going to church. Some are frightened, some curious, some move out of their homes, others treat their phantoms like a family pet. Reactions are individual, but what matters is that, day in and day out, ordinary people all over the region are seeing hearing, sometimes smelling or touching, something that, according to our understanding of physics and chemistry, can't exist. It happens far too often for all the witnesses to be crazy, mistaken or lying. The vast majority of them must be telling the truth as they believe it.

So, the rules must be wrong, or at least, incomplete. It is more than time for scientists to take account of people's experiences and evolve some new rules for us. Where will they begin? Some Victorian scientists spent their time with spiritualist mediums trying to prove that the dead can return or, at least, communicate. They gathered no evidence that this is the case, despite the common belief in Europe and North America that ghosts are the returned spirits of the dead.

It is easy to see why our primitive ancestors believed that the dead return. Living amidst and a prey to natural forces, they soon saw that nothing in nature is destroyed, only altered, and that the natural world is full of examples of death and re-birth. So the moon waxes and wanes, the sun retreats and advances, plants die in the winter and are reborn in the spring, fire changes wood to ash, cold turns water to ice, heat turns it to vapour. Hardly surprising that they came to believe that a human being can be reborn after death. If they saw visions of what seemed to be their dead relatives, this would only reinforce their belief.

Even so, centuries of this belief have left us no evidence that it is sound. On the contrary, we now know that the things that are changed naturally do not change back. Frogs do not turn back into tadpoles, nor butterflies become caterpillars, fossils do not turn back into living plants and animals. The explanation (or explanations) for what we call ghosts or paranormal events must lie elsewhere.

Michael Faraday is credited with the early laboratory work on induction and electro magnetism in the early 19th century. In the 1860s, the

German chemist Karl Reichenbach, announced the discovery of a new force which he named the 'odic' force and which would, he said, explain the phenomena of spiritualism. The British scientist, William Crookes, who had a deep interest in the paranormal, experimented with Reichenbach's odic force but got nowhere.

In the mid 1870s, the American inventor/engineer Edison rediscovered what he called 'a true unknown force' and began a series of experiments with the paranormal. Soon he concluded that his 'etheric' force was Reichenbach's 'odic' force, but his experiments went nowhere and, importantly to Edison, did not lead to his predicted cheapening of the electric telegraph system.

In 1889 Heinrich Hertz established the existence of high frequency electro magnetic waves, the phenomenon that both Reichenbach and Edison had stumbled on. Hertz realised the possibility of radio telegraphy but unlike his predecessors he did not make any connection with the paranormal.

In the 20th century scientists largely withdrew from the field to concentrate their research on commercial and military possibilities. Only a few brave souls took up the challenge of the paranormal. Thirty years ago one Dr Persinger in Canada collected accounts of 'anomalous incidents' from all over the world, everything from UFOs to sea serpents, and analysed his data to see if any patterns occurred.

He soon realised that reports of strange events seemed to cluster at times and places of electro magnetic disturbance, so he turned his research towards the effects of magnetic fields on the human brain. He established that the effect of quite low intensity magnetic fields on the frontal lobes of a human brain is to produce vivid and lifelike hallucinations together with by a loss of memory as to what had caused them. In other words, you could have a strange, lifelike, experience caused by magnetism and would believe that it was real.

At first he found that hallucinations revolved around the beliefs of the subject. Believers in Santa Claus might see him in their hallucinations, and believers in fairies or little green Martians might see them. His work continues and he has now developed a helmet which enables him to subject the wearer's frontal lobes to precise magnetic fields. In addition, he has learned how to stimulate particular ideas in the subject's mind so that he can almost guarantee the content of a hallucination.

We know now that the human brain contains an array of minute magnetic particles, though we do not know their purpose. Are they the receiver through which we experience what we call paranormal events? Is Dr Persinger on the brink of explaining a great deal about ghosts and other paranormal phenomena?

If the brain acts as a receiver, what might be the transmitter? We don't talk about haunted people but haunted places. And it seems to be true that in such places it is quite common for many people to have the same experience. Are these, ghosts, visions, hallucinations or whatever they are, somehow recorded in these places in electro magnetic form?

We repeat, this book is to convince laymen that they are not mad and to convince scientists that the answers really are out there, or in there.

Many thanks to all the helpful people who have provided us with their stories, and many apologies to those whose tales we could not fit in. Thank you also to Andy Tew who provided the pen and ink illustrations. Providing pictures for a book about ghosts is not easy, as our final chapter shows, and it was good to have Andy's support to liven up the acres of print.

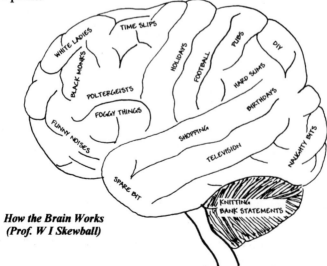

*How the Brain Works*
*(Prof. W I Skewball)*

# Birmingham

## Some Kind of Demon
### (Castle Vale)

"I will never forget the night in 1979 when, at about 4 am, I was attacked by some kind of demon. I don't know how it got into my bedroom. The window would only open a few inches and if it came in through the door it would have had to have gone past my father, who was up at the time. Perhaps it came down the chimney, or perhaps it didn't need to enter like ordinary things.

At the bottom of my bed was a floorboard which if anyone walked on it would make a noise loud enough to wake me up. And that's what happened. I heard the floorboard 'bang', then in the pitch dark something jumped on my bed. It felt as big as a dog, but we didn't have any pets. I pulled the bedclothes over my head but whatever it was tried to pull them off. It put one of its claws down my back and scratched it, then disappeared.

I went into my father's room to find him fully awake and reading. I lifted my pyjama top to show him my bleeding back and he went into my room, but found nothing.

It has not happened again and I have never found any explanation. However, my mother told me that she once slept in this room and was wakened by something pulling off the bedclothes."

## A Family House
### (Sutton Coldfield)

"From 1970 to 1973 I lived in a house at Sutton Coldfield, but I was so unnerved by my experiences there that I refused to stay there alone.

I was in my fifties, a company director, with a beautiful, comfortable detached four bedroomed family house built in 1924. It was quite dilapidated when we bought it and needed complete redecorating. No structural alterations were necessary but there were a lot of repairs to be done, for example, four hundred new roof tiles.

One evening I was sitting in the lounge where we had a rack of antique plates, when suddenly all the plates started moving around. I found it quite frightening. A little time later we were in bed one evening when we heard a click, and the landing light went on. One of the features of the house that we liked was that each door had a little diamond window of coloured glass, and it was very unnerving to have light suddenly flooding through it at 11.30 pm. My wife said, 'Are you going down to see who it is?' and I said, 'In a minute.'. I did eventually pluck up courage to go downstairs but nobody was about. We didn't think that much about it. We were on the main A38 road and that was before the Sutton Coldfield bypass was built, so all the traffic went past our door. We put it down to the vibrations of a heavy lorry.

On another occasion I saw the figure of a grey lady gliding into our back bedroom. Although I say grey, she was really more white or without colour, as if I was looking at a black and white TV. Although she was slightly transparent you could see her quite clearly. I would say that she was in her mid twenties and about 5 feet 8 inches tall. She was wearing, to the best of my knowledge, a high necked Edwardian dress which went down to the floor and trimmed with lace round the bottom. It had leg of mutton sleeves with lacy cuffs. I followed her into the bedroom but she had disappeared. This happened twice, with an interval of a few months.

This particular ghost, or whatever it was, only seemed to appear when I was there alone and never when my wife was at home. I got the feeling that she didn't like men.

One day I was working in the front garden when a car drew up on the road. It was someone who had lived in the house previously, not the person I bought it from but the man before that. We began chatting and I knew he was genuine because I had seen the heights of his children pencilled on the wall before I redecorated. He said that he had landscaped the garden and would I mind showing him round. While we were strolling he said, quite out of the blue, 'Have you seen the ghost yet?'. Obviously I wasn't the only person to see it. We compared details and his description was exactly the same as mine.

# "..not a nice atmosphere."
## (Bournville)

Sue Price's* experience happened about nine years ago when she went to visit her friend, Caroline Walker*, who lived on the Cadbury Village Trust estate in Bournville.

"Halfway through the evening I went up to the bathroom and I had only been there a couple of minutes when I realised I was looking at the light pull cord. It was swinging to and fro really fast, as if someone was pushing it. I felt frightened and my heart was pounding. My friend's son was then aged about 9 and his bedroom was next to the bathroom. A noise was coming from his room as if he was sorting through his toys looking for something. I shot downstairs quickly and found that the boy was sitting there.

I must have looked startled because my friend asked if I was alright. The way she said it made me suspect that she knew something strange had happened. I didn't know then that she was aware of something in the house, and I thought it was just me. I didn't say anything at the time and it wasn't until after she had moved out of the house that I heard about their problems."

Caroline* fills in the background.

"We didn't tell anyone what happened in that house until we had moved out and everything was behind us.

When we first went to live there in 1987 I said that I didn't like the feel of the house, it wasn't a nice atmosphere. The first thing that happened was that I was standing in the doorway talking to my husband when he said, 'The door's opening behind you'. At the time, I didn't think much of it. Another early incident was that we heard an upstairs window banging against the wall. Those windows were quite difficult to open with the kind of latch that you had to click to. My son was then about 8 years old and I thought he must have been larking about, but when I went into his bedroom he was fast asleep.

As the weeks went by the problems increased. It would go quiet for a month or two then everything would start up again. Doors and windows would open and close, slowly, and for no reason. Articles would disappear. For example, I would do a piece of ironing, put it on top of my washing basket and when I looked for it would be halfway down the basket. Some items disappeared altogether, such as the spare car keys which we have never found. Then, pictures would fall off the wall. I had a grandmother clock and the door was fastened by a hook, but it would swing open.

We had blocked in a fireplace and to make it look nice I placed an aspidistra on the hearth. I was on the phone one day when all the leaves suddenly bent to the one side, as if someone had pushed against it. One evening, I was sitting in the front room where I had an open display cabinet, when a Victorian cup flew across the room. Another time I heard a noise from my son's room as if someone was playing marbles, but when I went up he was fast asleep.

I had a cross collie dog which I would shut in the living room, but when I came back he would be in the front bedroom. The doors were the old-fashioned kind where you had to turn the handles to open them, so the dog could not have done it by himself.

Quite often I would see the dark shape of a dog on the stairs. It was quite big, I would say an Alsatian cross, though I didn't take that much notice.

Once I caught a quick glimpse of a shadowy figure on the stairs, a little bent old man with a hunch back. My son used to say that he could see the shadow of a man, then one night he shouted downstairs, 'There's somebody here.'. My mother rushed upstairs and she saw the little old man too. She came down and said, 'He's right you know.'.

We tried to find out who had lived in this place in the past. Ordnance Survey maps showed that before the houses were built the area was just farmland, but we did find quite a lot of pottery in the garden and some clay pipes. The only thing we could think of was that the little old man was a farmer.

My mother said that she didn't like the look of him so we decided to move, and quickly. We had lived there for three years but really couldn't stand any more."

*****

There seem to be two different types of paranormal event in this story. The swinging lamp cord, disappearing car keys and hidden ironing seem typical of the mischievious, provocative behaviour of a poltergeist. On the other hand the dog and the old man seem more like the type of image associated with particular buildings or places. These often turn out to be people or animals who once lived or worked there. Read on, and preferably read our other two books as well, *Midland Ghosts & Hauntings* and *Midland Spirits & Spectres*, both published by QuercuS. We suggest this (a) because it will cheer up our bank managers, and (b) so that you will see that most accounts of paranormal events fall into certain fairly clear groups.

# The White Lady
## (Castle Bromwich)

Castle Bromwich Hall was built in 1557 and 1558 by Sir Edward Devereux as a plain, single storey house. A hundred years later it was purchased by Sir John Bridgeman, the son of the Keeper of the Great Seal of England, who developed the building as befitted the offspring of such an important person. The Bridgemans were created Barons Bradford in 1792 and Earls of Bradford in 1815.

During the late 1970's Ray worked there as a Security Guard.

"When I went to work at a firm called Sword Security, we used to look after Lady Bradford's house, Castle Bromwich Hall. It was an attractive place. In what is now the Board Room there is a ceiling which is so beautiful, and it's in the same condition as when it was first put up. The gardens did suffer some neglect but have recently been restored.

*The baroque frontage of Castle Bromwich Hall with close up of the doorway.*

We used to patrol the grounds two or three times each night. After 6 o'clock in the evening we would patrol at 10, 11 or midnight and in the early hours of the morning; we used to vary the times. We had to go round the big rhododendron bushes and then round the back of the house. I was walking through at 12 o'clock one night when I saw a flash in front of me, and there was an elderly woman with long hair down to her shoulders wearing a long grey dress and with three Dalmatian dogs. I could not see her very clearly because she was mainly in silhouette and like a hazy black and white television picture. As soon as the vision appeared, it vanished.

I just froze. It doesn't matter how old you are or how strong, it sends a chill down your spine. I tried to light a cigarette but I was shaking so much I couldn't light it. I was also terribly cold, as though I had just come out of a deep freeze. When you are walking round in the dark you do imagine things, but I didn't imagine that woman.

The same security firm also looked after Solihull Library and for a period they held an exhibition about Castle Bromwich. It told you the history of Lady Bradford's house, and the story goes that her husband killed her. After the murder he took some bricks out of an alcove and bricked her up. For two or three days the dogs kept whining, so he took out some more bricks and put them in too."

✶✶✶✶✶

Although the white lady of Castle Bromwich Hall is a traditional local ghost, the tale that she was a murdered Lady Bradford is not likely to be true for two reasons. The first is that it fails to appear in any of the official records, the second is that Castle Bromwich Hall was usually let out, and it was only occupied by the Bradford family between 1775-9 and 1819-20. This is not to doubt Ray's account of what he experienced, only to say that it must have some other explanation.

# The Hunting Lodge
## (Sutton Park)

"In 1976 my husband and I took over the Bracebridge Cafe in Sutton Park. The nearest entrance was the Four Oaks Gate. It had once been Henry VIII's hunting lodge and was picturesque but antiquated, with oil and calor gas. It was really quiet down there, very remote. My husband was a drummer and played in a band so he was out until late some evenings. My daughter lent me her collie dog to keep me company.

The following incidents occurred in the winter of 1977. I was on my own one night and had just settled down in bed with the collie on the floor by my side, when I saw, lit up in the window, the face and regalia of Henry VIII, all glowing. I thought to myself, 'Now don't be silly' and I turned round to see the face of Henry on the wall behind me. The dog growled and went under the bed. I knew no one would believe that Henry VIII haunted the cottage so I didn't tell anyone. A couple of months later I said to my husband, 'I think we should move from here, this damp cottage isn't doing your bronchitis any good', and that's all I said.

A second incident happened a few months later, just before Christmas. My husband was very busy and wanted me to go out and help with the band, so my daughter did all the baking on Christmas Eve. The table in the kitchen was full of mince pies and food ready for the next day. When we got up in the morning the food had been thrown over the floor and all the mince pies were smashed. It couldn't have been the dog because my daughter had taken him home with her.

*The ornate Bracebridge Café in Sutton Park overlooks Bracebridge Pool.*

The third incident occurred just after my husband and I had got into bed one night. We both heard the noise of horses' hooves coming from the area where the stables used to be (we had converted the stables into a new kiosk). Then we heard a sound like great big boulders rolling down the brook which runs alongside the cellar. The tanks in the kitchen started filling up with water, although nobody was running it. The noise was terrible, we had never heard such a noise in our lives. A door from the kitchen leads into the lounge and we heard footsteps going through the kitchen, then the lounge door handle being tried. We pushed all the furniture against the door to barricade ourselves in and phoned the police. They didn't come straight away because they couldn't locate the spare key to the park gates. When they did arrive, there was no sign of anything, no break in, no footprints in the muddy ground outside, nothing.

Eighteen months later my husband came home, collapsed and died. He was only 45 and had been in good health."

# A Pot Bellied Man
## (Central Birmingham)

Mary Harvard* told us:

"I think all children are frightened of the dark at sometime or other. During the black out of World War II my mother liked us to go to bed in the dark. When we said we were frightened she would tell us that we must never be frightened in the dark, because whatever is there in daylight is there in the dark. And Mum used to say that it was a ghost who saved her life and that of her brother, Uncle Fred.

She used to live in a little two rooms up and two down house in Station Street, off Hurst Street, Birmingham. She was very poor because my father had TB and she had been disinherited by her family. I can't remember how many children there were, 4, 5 or 6, but they all slept in the one bed, mother and Uncle Fred at the head and the younger children at the foot. They were lying in bed when mother was woken up by the rattling of the bed rail. Standing at the foot of the bed was a large, pot bellied man with a gold fob chain. She grabbed Uncle Fred and ran screaming to her parents' room.

Her parents ran across the landing and told them, 'There's a man in my room'. Her father and mother inspected the bed and said that she was dreaming. Two or three children were still sleeping at the foot of the bed, but the chimney breast behind the headboard had collapsed, showering the head of the bed with bricks and masonry. When she described the man in great detail her parents said that it sounded like their grandfather. Because her mother had been disinherited there were no photographs or pictures of her grandfather in the house. If she had been in the bed she would have been showered in bricks, and that is how the ghost saved her life. He never appeared again."

# The Mysterious Chef
## (Central Birmingham)

"I don't believe in ghosts, but I had a strange experience in a Birmingham hotel. Do you know the Imperial in Temple Street? I worked there in the kitchens as a porter and one day I was upstairs doing a banquet. The chef sent me downstairs to collect some items. As I came down through the corridor, I saw the chef at the bottom of the stairs as plain as can be. I went upstairs and he was there. I said to him, 'You got downstairs quickly, how the hell did you manage it? You beat me coming down'. He said that he hadn't left the room.

I found out by talking to the others that the motel next door had burned down and the chef was burned to death, so perhaps I saw the chef from that motel."

# Sparky's Magic Piano
## (Digbeth, Birmingham)

John Sparky is well known in the Midlands as a pianist and piano dealer, but he has a second interest. His ancestor, William Sly, is thought by some people to be the real William Shakespeare. John is convinced that this is so, and has written a book to prove it. William Sly was a Birmingham man, so at his shop in Digbeth High Street John has staged an exhibition about him. John says:

"It's going very well. We have had over 5,000 visitors so far and most of them have signed the book saying that they think William Sly could be William Shakespeare. There's a portrait of William Sly in Shakespeare's daughter's house.

Since we opened the exhibition we have had a friendly ghost which arrived as soon as we brought in two old, wooden beams as part of the display. A local pub which is associated with Shakespeare has the reputation of being haunted. It was being redeveloped and they were going to put some old beams on the skip, so I asked if I could have them. I put the beams in two separate rooms but the ghost seems mainly to be in one of them.

Half a dozen of our visitors have remarked that they have heard a piano playing in this room when nobody is there. The piano tuner has heard it, so has a lady buying a piano and also a chap who comes in to help me.

I myself have heard it. One morning I was in the yard moving a piano with my son and a chap who plays the guitar when they said, 'There's a piano playing in there'. I said, 'It can't be, there's nobody there'. I went into the room to check and sure enough, it was empty.

The music is in the old fashioned style, not a tune you would recognise, it just sounds as if somebody is tinkering about on a piano. Not *Top of the Pops* or anything like that."

# The Phantom on the Landing
### (RAC Building, Edgbaston)

Dennis Arrowsmith started work for the RAC in 1977.

"The regional head office was in Hagley Road, Five Ways, an old building four or five storeys high. If you walked out of one room onto the landing there was an area 6 or 7 steps long where it was always freezing cold. I made some enquiries but there seemed absolutely no reason for this.

Bill Reeves was a great friend of mine. He worked Link 6 and I worked Link 7, which meant that we worked the same area and our shifts went one after the other. We both used to work well past our shift time and would sit and chat. One day he told me that he had seen the ghost of a man on the landing, and another employee, John Jones, categorically stated that he had seen a phantom man there.

Once a girl on night duty saw a man hanging from a beam in the same place. She was in a terrible state and had to be sent home because she couldn't work. I was told that a man had been found hanged on this landing years before."

✳✳✳✳✳

Coincidentally, a former security guard told us of a strange meeting in the building's car park. Just after twilight one evening he saw what he took to be an unauthorised person lurking on the car park and challenged them. The figure, which had been stooping, straightened up to reveal itself as a misty, grey apparition with a frightening face partly visible under a hood. It emitted a hissing sound and began to move towards our informant, who decided that discretion is a valuable part of security and withdrew, rather rapidly.

It is unusual for misty apparitions and the like to have any interaction at all with living humans, let alone to threaten them. Of all the accounts of the paranormal in this book and our two others, virtually the only 'things' that do interact are poltergeists, which direct obvious malice at certain people.

# Ghost in the Garden
## (Hodgehill, Castle Bromwich)

Margaret keeps a lot of animals and one Saturday morning in August 1988 she ran out of milk for the cats.

"I usually go shopping on a Friday night but that Friday my daughter had gone out and couldn't take me. First thing in the morning I thought, 'I'll just pop to the shops and get some'. Next door is a very nice house with a bay window, a circular step and a large tub of flowers, and my neighbour was out fussing with the tub. She was wearing a blouse, a waistcoat and an old fashioned hat. I called out to her, 'Hullo Mary*' but she didn't answer - she is a bit deaf. Then she just went. I assumed she'd gone to put the weeds somewhere.

I walked up the drive towards the shops and who did I see, but my next door neighbour coming back towards her house. She had been to visit another neighbour. I didn't tell her that I'd just seen her, she would have thought I was mad.

Later that day I said to her, 'Can I come in for a minute' and told her what had happened. She went white and said, 'That was my mother you saw, she looked just like me and she always wore this old fashioned hat'. Her mother had died about a year before I moved into my house. I said, 'Do you think she was following you?' and she replied, 'Oh no, she was always gardening'.

One morning seven or eight days later my neighbour came to my door at about 8.15. She said, 'I thought I must tell you, I was just on the telephone when somebody grabbed my arm and it was my mother's ghost.' She said that her mother had really held on to her arm and seemed to be trying to tell her something.

Afraid that her mother was trying to warn her of something, she went to be checked over by the doctor, who said that she had high blood pressure."

# The Late Tom King
## (Kingstanding)

Tony Robins is a plumber.

"One May about fifteen years ago I was doing some work at the top end of Endhill Road, the part that's a cul-de-sac. You only have to go down a little cutting and you're on the Chester Road.

I was working for a woman aged about 65 and her daughter who lived alone. One day I got to the house and the old lady was frightened to death. She hadn't mentioned anything to her daughter because she didn't want to frighten her, but she told me all about it. She had been sitting in the lounge reading at about 9 o'clock in the evening when a figure had come out of the wall and glided across the room. It was about seven feet tall and wearing a black cape and tricorn hat. It had blazing red eyes and looked at her as it passed.

She told me about it in the May, and in the November I read something in the *Evening Mail* that made my blood run cold. A lorry driver had seen a dark figure, described as a highwayman, not fifty yards from my customer's house, and it had been going in the same direction. I know that she hadn't said anything to anybody except me. There is a legend that the highwayman, Tom King, who was a friend of Dick Turpin, haunts that part of the Chester Road."

✳✳✳✳✳

Tom King was born locally near Stonnal, and he was indeed a friend and working partner of Dick Turpin. It is said that Turpin, not recognising King, held him up, but King did recognise Turpin and suggested a partnership. They operated together with great success but mainly in Epping Forest. The Chester Road was one of the three worst in the Midlands for highwaymen between the mid 17th and late 18th centuries, but we cannot trace any evidence that Tom King ever worked it.

According to one story, the infamous partnership ended due to an unhappy accident. The landlord of the Green Man at Epping took hold of King, intending to arrest him for the theft of a horse. King called on

Turpin to shoot the innkeeper, but Turpin's shot killed King. Another account has it that King was arrested and burnt to death for his crimes in Sutton Park, but this is not true.

In *Midland Spirits & Spectres* we mentioned the local legend that a ghostly highwayman rides across the park at dusk, crosses Icknield Street and the Chester Road into Sutton Oak Road heading for the Parson & Clerk pub. From accounts of various sightings he appears to be a young man wearing a mask, a tricorn hat and black cape.

# The Edwardian
## (Moseley)

"The most terrifying thing that ever happened to me", John Lewis told us, "was when my wife and I lived in Moseley. We had a very nice flat in a three storey house on the site of some old stables. The bottom flat was occupied by a mother and daughter and we were very friendly with them.

One Sunday morning the mother came up to our flat as white as a ghost. She was in quite a state. 'Whatever is the matter?', we asked, but she wouldn't say; she told us that we would only laugh. When she calmed down she said it was about her daughter and it seemed she had come up to see if we had any suggestions.

Evidently strange things had been going on for some time but it had come to a head the previous evening. The daughter had an L-shaped room and her bed was the far end from the door. She woke up and the room was in darkness except for the street lights, but she could see a man in Edwardian clothes standing at the bottom of the bed. He had no face. She was petrified. She tried to call out to her mother but was paralysed with fear. However, the switch to her bedside lamp was on a flex under the pillow, and she managed to switch it on. With that, the figure disappeared like smoke. The daughter went into the mother and asked if she could get into bed with her.

I suggested that she should see the vicar of St Agnes's church at Moseley and asked them to let me know if anything else happened. One day she flew up the stairs shouting, 'It's here.'. I ran down the stairs and the three of us (mother, daughter and myself) entered the room.

There was a large cross which they had made out of straw. The room was very cold and I had only been there for a couple of seconds when the daughter gave a shriek and ran out, she had evidently seen the apparition. I felt a kind of coldness which moved around me. The girl was later able to draw a picture of this man and it was very distinctive, with an Edwardian style watch in his waistcoat pocket.

The Bishop of Birmingham came out twice to exorcise the flat and I remember seeing him in all his regalia."

✶✶✶✶✶

Notice how many of these reports include a reference to coldness, and see the next one.

# The Maid
## (Moseley)

Sylvia* prefers to appear under a pseudonym in telling this story:

"No one believes me although I'm a very down-to-earth person. In about 1972 I was at my sister in law's house, a very large old place in Moseley. I was cleaning the top storey where the maid had once lived and which now housed a guest room and bathroom. Having cleaned it I walked across a gallery landing and I had very nearly reached the top of the stairs when I heard a sudden whoosh sound and felt a real coldness.

I turned icy cold. The noise made me turn round and I saw what I can only describe as a tall, thin grey figure, a solid grey opaque mist. She was dressed in Edwardian clothes with a plain skirt down to the ground, as if she were a maid. She had no head. She walked from the bathroom to the guest room then disappeared, but was clearly visible for about three seconds. I assume that the apparition wanted me to know she was there and wanted me to see her. I told my husband but he just laughed.

I wasn't the only one who saw her. My sister in law was in her late 70s and after her mother died she wouldn't go upstairs to bed. She had to have day and night nurses. One of them phoned me one day about quite another matter, something concerning my sister in law, then she said out of the blue,

'This house is haunted, you know'. I said to her, 'What makes you say that?'. She said, 'I have seen her, a little old lady on the stairs. So have other nurses'. I said, 'Well, I have to admit that I have seen her as well'.

I assume that was the reason my sister in law wouldn't go upstairs. We had to keep it quiet because some of her nurses were very superstitious. It seems that years before my relatives had given their maid a hard time and treated her like dirt. I think she came back to haunt them, particularly my sister in law.

It was a very dark house and you could easily imagine things but I know that I didn't imagine this."

# The Mourners
## (Northfield)

Two years ago Joan Pointer* moved into a hundred year old house which needed quite a lot of repairs.

"The first strange thing occurred on a lovely autumn day, sunny and bright with no frost. I said to my daughter in law, 'I'll just pop to the post office'. I went upstairs to get my coat and as I was coming down the stairs again I put my hand in my pocket and thought, 'What's this, a pocket full of ice'. I went into the kitchen and asked my daughter to put her hand in my pocket. She asked me, 'What are you going to do?'. 'Nothing,' I said, 'just put your hand in my pocket'. She did so and said, 'You've got ice in your pocket.'. I said, 'Thanks, that's all I wanted to know'.

Things went on from there. There was a tapping on the wall which would get louder and louder. My daughter lives in Walsall and asked me to phone when it started. When I did she couldn't hear the noise at first, but it got louder and she did hear it. She said, 'Tell it to go away'. I said 'Go away.' really loudly, and suddenly the bedroom door slammed shut. After these episodes the alarm always went off at 10 minutes to 3 in the morning, no matter what time it was set for.

A strange smell would come and go, and on one occasion smoke appeared from nowhere and drifted across the bedroom. I saw an apparition of a man on the landing and the same man in my bedroom by the dressing table. I heard the footsteps of several people walking across the room; the sound was very clear because we had no carpets down. One night I woke up and there were mumbling voices downstairs.

Another night round the end of my bed I saw people of all different shapes and sizes. I had somebody come in and take photographs and the only thing that showed up was a face at the end of the cot in my bedroom. My neighbours told me that in the old days, when anybody died, the mourners gathered round the bottom of the bed. The bedroom was such a shape that you could only ever have put a bed where my bed was. People said that I was seeing and hearing these old mourners."

✻✻✻✻✻

So perhaps in hearing and seeing the people in and around the bedroom Joan has been experiencing some kind of replay of a traumatic event. However, the ice, the tapping and the derangement of the alarm clock seem unconnected, as if something else is going on.

# The Phantom Nurse
## (Northfield)

In 1990 Beryl was having her toes straightened as a private patient at the Woodlands Hospital, Northfield. She was in her own room.

"What they do is to push a kind of nail through your toe and then put a cork on the end of it to warn people not to touch. It's so painful and they don't put any bedclothes over your feet.

Some hours after my operation I woke up to see my toes sticking out of the bottom of the bed. Standing right beside them with her hands clasped together was this lady. I realised immediately that it was the sister because she was wearing a sister's uniform, with a frilly cap and a little bow under the chin. She had a pleasant, rounded face with round glass spectacles and she looked quite happy. She was about average height, and, I would say, a bit cuddly.

She looked down at my toes, nodded thoughtfully - and went. I thought, 'This is strange', but I wasn't frightened. I think I nodded off to sleep. The next day I woke up and there she was again. The second time she moved slightly and smiled. I could see her clear as day and I would know her again. I thought, 'I don't know if I believe in ghosts'.

When a nurse came in I asked her, 'Do you believe in ghosts?', and she asked, 'Why?'. I started to tell her about my visitor but she interrupted me. 'Don't say another thing, I'm fetching my friend'. They returned a few minutes later and as I told them, they were both gobsmacked. I had given an exact description of what one of the nurses had seen. She said to the other, 'There you are, and you laughed at me when I told you.'

The nurse said that she was supposed to be looking after someone who had just come round from anaesthetic but started to doze off. Suddenly she felt someone tapping her on her shoulder. The phantom sister was rebuking her for going to sleep, standing there wagging a finger.

The sister's photograph was supposed to be somewhere in the hospital, though I never saw it. She never married and was devoted to her patients. If I went into a room full of photographs I could pick out the sister who came to visit me."

# Strange Visitors
## (Stirchley)

Most people never see anyone who is not actually, physically, there, but if they do it is a once in a lifetime event. Some people with psychic abilities may see someone three or four times during their lives, but Mandy Brown* has these strange experiences all the time.

"I don't think of myself as special or different from other people, and I would say that, rationally, I don't believe in the paranormal.

I consider that these experiences fall into two categories. In the first I sense people more than I can see them. I feel that they are there and I can see them out of the corner of my eye, but when I turn to look at them, they go. You might be concentrating on something, following a train of thought, then suddenly realise that this person is on your shoulder and start talking about something else. Then you go back to what you were doing. You don't think about things one at a time so your thought processes haven't moved at all, one line of thought has just switched for a moment. Only when you go back do you realise that something is different.

The second type of experience is when I see somebody that nobody else can see. I'm just pottering away, doing my own thing, and bang, somebody will appear. Once it has happened you are aware that it has happened, but I usually take it for granted at the time. It seems quite real and it is only after the event that I realise that the person wasn't exactly there. It is a continual frustration and it does frighten me, in fact it freaks me out. But I tell myself I am being silly and I can control it. If I tell them to go, then they do go.

I see people that I don't know at all, people that I know slightly and others that I know very well, such as members of the family. Sometimes ancestors whom I never met when they lived appear and make themselves known to me, usually when I am distressed. They say, 'We are concerned about you'. I say, 'I don't want you here, you are frightening me, please go away.', and they go.

The first experience that I found really frightening and made me want to disassociate myself from it, was when I was 11 years old. After my grandmother died she came to visit me every night before I went to sleep. But then, in my dreams, I would go back to the maisonette where she used to live. I would levitate up to the balcony, the door would be open and I would go inside. The kitchen was on the left and my grandmother would be there, saying, 'Come in, come in.'. But I wouldn't go in. I would go out to the balcony and back down. This happened every night for a couple of months.

I have seen a certain young woman almost since my childhood. She wears a long skirt with a bustle. She has a bodice with a row of rectangular jet beads down the front. Her hair is taken back round her ears and piled high on the back of her head. She talks to me and she can be a real cow. I sense her nearly all the time, although I have no idea who she is.

My father in law lived in Edinburgh and for years suffered from Alzheimer's Disease. A couple of months before he died my brother in law, who was living in Durham, saw an apparition of him. At this point I started going up to Durham and every time I went there he would turn up, even after he had died. My husband saw him too. The weirdest thing was that when he appeared he would be very young, in his twenties, and tall, although he was not a tall man. He now appears to me at Stirchley and tries to talk to me, but I can't understand what he is going on about. Last time he said that I had got to tell somebody something about his daughters, the sisters. I told him that I couldn't understand and he went.

A few years ago I had to go into hospital and was very unhappy because I was in a mixed ward. Before my operation I was muttering and not settling down when somebody came in and sat on my bed. I distinctly saw the bed depressed. Then I saw that Mick, an old friend of mine, was sitting there looking at me. I said, 'Oh, you have turned up.' and I went on, 'By the way, you're dead, aren't you?' I was lying in bed, talking to him and I couldn't have cared less what everyone thought. Mick often appears and he usually tells me to give up smoking. He's one of those that I usually see out of the corner of my eye. I don't mind him, I can accept people that I know and members of the family.

Sometimes these people give me a wonderful feeling of happiness. When I was a child we went to visit a stately home in Warwickshire. As soon as I walked into the first room I saw a woman running towards me with her arms out in pure joy, as if she knew me. I thought, 'I'll recognise you in a moment.', but then she disappeared.

At other times I get a horrible feeling. Recently, in an exhibition of old photographs, there was a picture of a drunken woman. That gave me a really nasty experience. I had an overwhelming feeling of wanting to say, 'You don't understand, you don't know why I became like this.', as if it were me in the picture. I don't think that should have been on display.

I think my daughter is going to be the same. The father of my friend Sue* died and with my daughter, then 4 years old, I went to stay with her for a few days. At one point my daughter came downstairs, saying, 'I've just been talking to Sue's dad. I have to go back upstairs now to say good-bye to him because he's going.' She had never met Sue's dad and she didn't know that he had recently died.

It is my belief that these experiences are there for everybody but people are simply too busy to link into them."

# Something Fishy
## (Witton)

Sylvia Knight* lives near the Aston Villa ground and the cemetery, though neither of these neighbours seems to have much bearing on her strange experiences.

"I'm haunted by a horrible fish smell which began about 7 or 8 years ago. We knocked down a wall which was part of a staircase to open up the hallway, and this smell just seemed to come out of the wall. At the time I didn't think much about it. I thought next door must be cooking fish or something, then I wondered if it was coming up from the ground. I still haven't found a solution and I've tried anything and everything.

The smell affects an area about a yard across and it stays in one spot at a time. You can walk out of it, then turn round and walk back into it again. Sometimes it lasts a few fleeting seconds but at other times it has lingered for as long as twenty minutes. The smell is mainly at the top of the stairs or the bottom of the landing. It sometimes goes into the bedrooms although it has only once been in my bedroom. My family can smell it and they say, 'You're friend's here again'.

Some friends of mine who are into this kind of thing told me to try talking to 'him', that is the smell. When I did this it started to follow me. It doesn't actually travel behind me but it turns up in the places that I'm going to. It will be on the landing, then when I go into the kitchen it's there.

It has followed me to all kinds of places, several times it's followed me to work. It has always been a bit of a joke among people there that I have a ghost. One day a woman walking down the stairs said, 'There's a horrible smell of fish here', to which I answered, 'Yes, that's my ghost.' Once it followed me next door to a party there where it went all round the room meeting people.

The smell went away for about eighteen months and then came back again. I can think of no reason at all why it should disappear for eighteen months and it didn't seem to coincide with anything. I know several people who didn't believe in ghosts but after experiencing mine they have changed their minds."

✳✳✳✳✳

Sylvia seems remarkably collected and cheerful about something which would drive most of us to distraction, but hers is not the only case of a so called psychic aroma. In *Midland Ghosts & Hauntings* we reported three stories. *The Pilot* was a cigarette smoking wartime RAF officer who appeared to a lady in Ironbridge. *Pungent Tobacco* involved a house at Upton Snodsbury in Worcestershire where a friendly but invisible resident enjoys a pipe. Leamington Spa was the setting for *Mignonettes & Clarissa*, a richly detailed and wonderful story of the sweet scent of those flowers and the appearance of a young woman who seemed to belong to about 1915. In these cases the aromas were accompanied by the sight or felt presence of a person and other events, but unaccompanied scents are not unusual.

# The Grey Lady
# of Warley Park
## (Warley Woods, Bearwood)

The thousands of people who visit Warley Woods and Warley Park may be interested to know (if they haven't already seen it) that Warley Park has a famous ghost.

About 700 years ago much land in Warley was held by Lady Joan de Somery, the sister of Margaret de Somery who inherited Dudley Castle. She was a very devout woman and when she died in 1325 she bequeathed her property to the monks at Halesowen Abbey on condition that they prayed eternally for her soul. She also stipulated that the rents from the land should be distributed annually to the poor. The monks would not have liked that.

All went well until in 1535 Henry VIII dissolved the monasteries, and in the looting of ecclesiastical treaures and buildings that followed Halesowen Abbey was destroyed. All this meant that the prayers for the welfare of Joan's soul had to be discontinued, and (the story goes), an angry Joan returned to this world. Whatever you think of this explanation, there is no doubt that many people have reported seeing a spectre in the Park.

Nightly hauntings of the area by a Grey Lady became so frequent that in 1822 she was cited in a murder trial. The body of a man who had died from head injuries had been found in Warley Woods. An acquaintance with whom he had quarrelled earlier in the day was accused of the murder but defended himself by pointing out that the deceased had been riding a horse in an area well known for the appearances of Joan's ghost. The animal could have seen it, reared with fright and thrown its rider. Three men testified that the ghost was a regular visitor to the area.

Thirty years earlier the 110 acre Warley estate had been purchased by Samuel Galton, who managed to be both a Quaker and a gunmaker. He built a modest house but when he died his son decided he wanted a much more splendid residence, and in 1818 work began on Warley Hall. Built in a mediaeval gothic style it was more commonly known as Warley Abbey.

An extract from an illustrated local magazine of 1890 reads:

> "Warley Hall of course numbers a ghost among its traditions, it is called the Grey Lady of Warley ... The only tangible proof of her that now exists is a sketch that was done of her by Mr. Harry Furniss while he was a guest of Mr.Reid in March, 1888. Possibly the old lady knew that Mr, Furniss was an artist and with true womanly vanity wished to have her "picter took". At any rate she appeared on that occasion to the company at Warley Hall in the small hours of the night, just as they had got to the stump of their last cigar and the bottom of their toddy glasses, and their thoughts were wandering bedwards. The lights in the room burnt blue and then a marrow-freezing rapping at the door was heard, the door swung open noiselessly and the grey lady was seen with her hands uplifted and her head thrown back in quite a dramatic attitude. She remained just long enough to give Mr Furniss's eye an expression, and straight way Mr Furniss put down the ghost in pencil."

In spite of strenuous efforts we have not been able to trace a copy of the sketch.

In 1906 the Warley estate was purchase by public funds and opened to the citizenry as Warley Park. Warley Hall was used by the War Office during World War I but its state of disrepair grew worse until it fell down as much as it was pulled down, in 1957. However, the Grey Lady appears independently of the house, she was seen long before the house was built, has been seen many times in Warley Park and will no doubt continue to haunt the area for many years to come. Long live the Grey Lady, if we can put it like that.

Warley Park has more to offer, for during the 1900s the Grey Lady seems to have undergone a sex change. John Lewis writes about the days of his youth:

"Before Warley Abbey had been demolished I was with a friend of about the same age approaching Warley Park from the Barclay Road side. You went through an entrance and down a hill and then you came to Warley Abbey. It was a lovely summer's day with plenty of people about, more than today because people used to come to the woods from a long distance.

My friend and I were chatting away happily about this and that and certainly not talking about ghosts, when we both saw a monk. He was about 30 yards away and came out of the side of Warley Abbey. We stopped and looked at each other. We could not believe our eyes. It was obvious that no monk should be there, and we ran as near as we could to get a closer look. The monk walked, or rather glided, along the side of the building then round towards the front. We could not see his face because at first he was too far away but then as we got closer we only saw the sideways view. He looked very real, youngish and slim in a brown habit. He was there for two or three minutes but then grew fainter and fainter until he disappeared altogether."

We can't imagine why a monk should lurk round a 19th century building just because it was built in a gothic style, but there you go.

# Pinfield Farm
## (Yardley)

Michael Hunt, secretary of the Vale of Evesham Historical Society and a friend of Seba Mansfield, offered us this account.

"To the west of Yardley Cemetery and just north of the Grand Union Canal is Mansfield Road. It is named after the Mansfield family who once owned Pinfield Farm on which the surrounding housing estates were built. During the early years of the 20th century the farmhouse was occupied by Seba Mansfield, his parents, his sisters and his Aunt Annie.

The prim and proper Victorian Aunt was usually dressed in a crinoline. She seems to have been the moneyed member of the family and used to sit and count her hoard in her lap. Down the garden there was an ancient apple tree from which she insisted on having the first fruit as her right. When Annie died the apple tree died and on the morning after her death was found fallen across the garden.

Conditions at Pinfield Farm were very primitive and the loo was down the garden, a three seater with large, medium and small holes, but no flush. One night Aunt Annie was treading carefully in the direction of the loo carrying a candle when the light attracted a marauding owl. The bird swooped down on the candle and Aunt Annie and the result was much the same as seeing a ghost because Aunt Annie fled into the safety of her kitchen.

Pinfield Farm had the reputation of being haunted. Seba's sisters insisted upon sleeping together and often referred to bumps in the night and other noises.

On one occasion guests were entertained overnight. It was a large building, on the first floor there was a long gallery type of landing with bedrooms off, and there was a bedroom on either side of the stairs. Two couples were accommodated in rooms at either end of the landing. That night, after everyone had gone to bed and were sound asleep, the visitors were awakened by loud bumps and bangs on the landing. They rushed to their bedroom doors, flung them open, and found themselves gazing at each other. There was nothing visible to cause the noises, which by then had ceased.

With her money Aunt Annie built three shops or houses in Yardley Road and moved into number 263. Seba's father let the farm to a tenant and the family joined her there.

The new tenants of Pinfold Farm were a family with one senior member. On one occasion he was just making his nightly trek to the outside loo when on the path before him he saw a lady dressed in a crinoline. He forget his errand and returned to the house in a very frightened state. When the others investigated the old man's sighting the ghost had gone.

When Seba Mansfield's father was dying something very strange happened. His sister called to Seba that if he wanted to see his father alive then he should hurry to his bedside. Seba was too late and was standing grieving silently he heard a mighty rushing, rustling noise from the staircase. He opened the door to the stairs, and discovered that all of the wallpaper had fallen from the walls.

When both of Seba's parents had died he and his sisters decided to sell the farm and its contents. It was a sad day. Gone was all the paraphernalia of a Victorian farmer, the duck guns, powder flasks, four poster beds, tables and chairs - all sold. When the enormously heavy sideboard was removed the word 'wait' was found written backwards in chalk. Seba's sister wiped it away but it returned, and despite other attempts to erase it, it remained.

The farm still stood by the canal when I last passed that way. There is no land, no fields, but I wouldn't like to say there was no ghost."

"Little Gordon's dyslexia was
not diagnosed for some time."

# Black Country

## Apparition in Profile
### (Hayley Green, Halesowen)

Mrs Lewis told us a strange story.

"In broad daylight one Sunday evening at about 5.30, I nodded off on the settee. When I woke up there was an apparition standing right beside me and looking down which gradually became clearer and clearer. It was transparent and through it I could see the chimney breast and the recess. It was in black and white, no colour, with wispy hair and slightly rounded shoulders. I thought, 'Oh golly!' The vision was there for a full minute and I recognised it as somebody I knew, but I couldn't think who. I said, 'Don't go, don't go yet, I want to know who you are.', but it gradually faded out in the same way that it had appeared.

I went upstairs and happened to pass our big mirror. Glancing sideways at myself I realised that the apparition was of me. My hair and everything were exactly the same. I hadn't recognised myself because the apparition was in profile, and it's not often you see yourself that way."

*****

According to tradition Mrs Lewis should have died shortly after seeing her own phantom. Alternatively, what we have here may be a curious example of an 'out of the body' experience where, for a change, it is the body that does the observing, not the distant spirit.

## Rattling the Ashes
### (Cradley Heath)

"Thirty years ago I had three small boys and when the youngest was 10 months old I was given a three bedroomed council house. It was a semi detached where the chimney breasts in each house backed onto one another, and if your next door neighbour raked the ashes of a coal fire with a poker you could hear it clearly. I had heard this rattling on several mornings and thought the old lady next door, Mrs Price, must have a coal fire.

My husband worked nights so I was alone. Three days after we moved in and after I had gone to bed, I heard the rattling again. I thought, 'I wish she would stop clearing the ashes at this time of night', then I turned over and went to sleep. A bit later I felt somebody sit on the bed and the springs go down. Startled, I sat up and looked around. A street lamp illuminated our bedroom and there, sitting on the bed, was a man. He was grey haired and elderly with a pot belly. He wore a grey vest and a white collarless grandad shirt which reached past his knees. He had other distinguishing features which I can't remember, but I think one of them was a monocle. I just said 'Bugger off.!', and he went.

I hadn't spoken to Mrs Price since we moved in as I was very busy with my three small children. However, the next day I said to her, 'I did have a funny experience last night, an old man sat on my bed'. She said, 'What was he like?' I told her and she went on to say that I had just described the man who used to live in the house. As an ex miner he was given a good supply of coal, and he would rattle the ashes every night. Mrs Price hadn't been using her coal fire. I asked her how long ago he had died and she said about fifteen or twenty years before. His widow had stayed on in the house and we had moved in after her. I never saw him again."

# The Spiral Staircase
## (Dudley Castle)

"On 10th October 1998 I went with a team to a ghost watch at Dudley Castle. We began at 12.15 am. Part of the Keep had been roped off but I cocked my leg over and went in there. As soon as I started to climb the spiral staircase I felt drowsy, sick, dizzy and nauseous. Something touched the back of my head, there was a tingling sensation in my face and something brushed me to one side.

At 2.30 am I returned to the staircase and climbed the stairs. The previous sensations returned. When I reached the top, I turned to come down but I felt someone tall and well built come up against me and, very quickly, put his hand in the small of my back and push me down the stairs.

*The keep of Dudley Castle. This is one of the most haunted places in the Midlands, as you can see in The Ghosts of Dudley Castle from our previous book, Midland Ghosts & Hauntings.*

When on a ghost watch you must never go anywhere alone and my friend, Wayne, had come with me. He said that I rose two feet into the air and flew down the stairs like an aeroplane, landing twelve or thirteen steps below. My back was badly cut and bruised and my hands grazed.

We were really scared and abandoned the watch."

# Nightmares
## (Netherton)

"I'm now at Birmingham University so this story goes back some years. When I was a small child I used to stay at weekends with my grandparents in Yew Tree Road. I usually slept in one bedroom but occasionally, I don't know why, they would put me in another.

There was something not quite right about the second room. It had a cold and clammy feeling and even in the middle of summer it was cooler than it should have been. I have a vague recollection of having terrible nightmares in there and seeing lots of flames. My mum said that when I was put to sleep in that room the bed would start vibrating, but I don't remember this. Apparently the bed also shook when my sister was put to sleep there. When I was old enough I was able to tell my grandparents that there was something odd about the room and that I didn't want to sleep there any more.

The story is that, during World War II when my grandfather was on leave from the forces, the woman next door accidentally set her house alight. Her clothes caught fire and she rushed out to the yard. My grandfather climbed the fence and doused the flames but she was seriously burned and died in hospital a few weeks later. My grandfather decided to buy her house and so they moved from the house in which they were living to next door. In later years he told me that the bedroom I disliked was probably the room in which the fire had started."

# Woman in a Hood
## (Walsall)

"On the corner of Bradford Street and Vicarage Lane stands a block of flats known as the Heritage. It was once Walsall's General Hospital (Sister Dora) and before that a workhouse. There were loads and loads of beds and the wards were in the form of a cross. The top floor was rather like a hospice is now, kept for the very sick patients, mainly cancer. The wards were very tiny and cramped.

I started nursing at the Walsall Hospital in the 1950's, before it was upgraded. I was only about 17 and one night I was sent to the top floor with a message. The wards were in darkness and at first I couldn't see anyone, but then I made out the black shape of someone with a hood. I couldn't see her clearly but she looked like the recent Scottish Widow's life assurance advertisement. I asked her if she knew where the sister was but she didn't answer and just glided off. I went back down on the lift and found the sister of the floor below. I said that I was looking for the sister of the upstairs ward. She told me that there were no staff up there at that moment. I said, 'I've just spoken to somebody' and she answered, 'Oh, that must have been the grey lady'."

# The Saving Hand
## (Walsall)

"In 1937 when I was about 12 we lived in Hospital Street, Walsall, opposite Sister Dora's isolation hospital. I caught pneumonia which developed into pleurisy and had to go into the Children's Hospital. Two ribs were removed and I went into a coma. As I came out of it the ward seemed full of beautiful light and wonderful music.

I recovered and, like all youngsters who have to convalesce, I got bored. Wandering down the entry, I went into the street and across the road. At that time the hospital had two great green gates in a high wall. I climbed the gates and sat on the wall, swinging my legs. Suddenly I fell. The wall was very high and I went down head first. By rights, I should have had a terrible head injury, but I felt a hand on my back and something held me upright until I reached the ground. That wasn't the only thing. At the bottom of the wall was a purse with a five shilling piece in it."

# The Haunted Bed
## (Wednesbury)

"When I was about 5 years old my parents moved to a new house. This was just after World War II in the early 1950s when money was short. They didn't really have enough money to furnish the house, but a friend offered them a large bed for me which had belonged to his father. The owner of the bed had been dead for some years, so I never met him. It was a fine piece of furniture, one of those beds with a headboard, a

footboard and curly springs. I had to climb up into it, and even at that age it seemed to have an overbearing presence.

One night I had been in bed for about thirty minutes when I was actually, physically woken up by a gentleman standing at the side of the bed saying, 'What are you doing in my bed?'. He was very dapper, but in different type of clothes to what people were wearing in the 1950s. He was somewhere in his mid 60s with his hair parted in the middle, short but extremely smartly dressed in a three piece suit. He wore quite a heavy watch chain and a stand up round collar which didn't come over the top of his tie. I was alarmed, I rolled to the other side of the bed and fell out. The noise alerted my parents and my mother came into the room asking, 'What is the matter?'. When I described the man Mother said, 'Don't be silly, it was only a dream', but I was sure it was real.

Some time later my mother realised that the apparition I had seen was the owner of the bed, an ironmonger who had owned a shop in Wednesbury. Mother had never met him but she happened to see photos of him. What was especially distinctive was the stand up round collar with the tie that didn't come over the top of it..

Not long after that my mother sold the bed and bought another one more suitable for a little lad of 6."

# The New House
## (Wednesbury)

"When we moved to a new house in Wood Green, Wednesbury, my daughter was 14. You know what they're like at that age, she didn't want to move and she was determined not to like the new house. We gave her a lovely little bedroom at the front and she did like it eventually, but it took two years, and for all that time she was very unhappy.

Whenever she came into the hall she said she could see water on the ceiling. I told her, 'I can't see any'. Another time she would say, 'I can still see some'. She would put things in her dressing table drawer and they would disappear. When she was 15 or 16 she would ask who had used up all the cotton wool from her drawer. She had an older brother and we asked him if he had moved it, but he replied that of course he wouldn't go into his sister's drawer, and of course he hadn't. I wondered if she was unconsciously taking it in the night, so I decided to try it for myself. I put a bag of cotton wool balls in her drawer and the next time I looked they had gone.

My son had a guitar which was usually propped against the bed, but one day when he went to work I could hear someone pulling hands across the strings. For a moment, I thought it was my son, then realised he was out. I went upstairs but his room was empty and the guitar was standing by the bed.

One morning I went to wake my daughter and as I did so she gave a funny little cry. She said, 'I was dreaming that Nan had fallen downstairs and broken her arm'. At 2 o'clock we had a telephone call to say that Nan had fallen and broken her arm, but it wasn't from falling downstairs. She had been taking a dinner round to her neighbour and there was a gate between the two houses where my husband had laid a board. The weather was icy and Nan had slipped on the board and broken her arm.

This sort of thing continued for two years, on and off, not enough to worry you but a bit at a time, then when my daughter had settled into the new house it stopped."

✷✷✷✷✷

This looks very much like poltergeist activity. We have described at least six cases in our previous books and you may find it interesting to compare them. The story above is a very mild example set beside the terrifying events in *The House over the Waters*, the last story in *Midland Ghosts & Hauntings*.

In the same book we mention the long history of poltergeists; in Britain they were recorded as early as 1188. They are usually associated with disturbed and unhappy people in a state of emotional stress.

# Cavaliers & Roundheads
## (Rushall Hall, Nr Walsall)

Rushall Hall, home of the Leigh family, was built as a fortified house in the 15th century during the Wars of the Roses. Two hundred years later during the Civil War the house and the church next to it were fortified and occupied by the Royalists. In May 1644 the Earl of Denbigh set out from Stafford to attack the Hall. On the 29th bombardment began and continued until 9 pm. The *Victoria County History* reports on 'Mistress Leigh defending it gallantly with only her men and her maids'. However, the Cavaliers decided to surrender on condition that they were allowed to march out alive without their arms and be 'conveyed' to Lichfield.

Mary Payton was born in Rushall. "My granny, Maggie Cunningham, worked at Rushall Hall in about 1910 as a cleaner.

In those days to reach the Hall from Rushall you had to cross fields belonging to the church. People have told me that they remember my granny running hell for leather across these fields, away from the Hall. Normally she wore her hair in a neat bun but on that occasion it was all over the place. She was wearing an apron made from old sacking, which is what they used to wear in those days, and carrying a bucket. She told everyone that while she was cleaning she had heard the rustle of a dress. Whatever it was, it frightened her so much that she never went back there again, though she badly needed the money.

My Uncle George also has a story about the Hall. He used to go dancing until late at night and would cut across the fields to go home. He swears that one night he saw the grey figure of a woman in front of him. He is quite a fearless man and he put out his hand to touch the figure, but it disappeared.

There are supposed to be bloodstains in the Hall that nobody can wash out. The story goes that during the Civil War some of the Cavalier officers, rather than let their women fall into the hands of the Cromwellians, disposed of them. There is a traditional ghost which is supposed to walk from the Hall across the fields to a pool now known as the Ladypool."

The last story about the disposing of the ladies is unlikely to be true because it does not appear in any of the official documents. Perhaps some of the gallant ladies were killed during the fighting and the Puritans, not wishing to be held responsible for their deaths and wishing to discredit the Royalists, spread the story that they had been killed by their officers.

It may be that the lady who walks the fields is the ghost of 18 year old Kitty Lyon, who was shot dead under the Cattle Bridge in the same meadow on a Sunday afternoon in September 1941. Her companion Violet Richards was also shot and savagely beaten by the killer. Further details of this crime (and a map of the area) can be found in *Midland Murders and Mysteries*, (Barrie Roberts, QuercuS, 1997).

# Grandfather's Room
## (Shortheath, Willenhall)

"My mother had six children and, as if she didn't have enough to cope with, when our grandparents grew too old to look after themselves they moved in with us. We lived in a large, rambling house called Sandbeds in the village of Shortheath.

41

My grandparents had a room upstairs until my grandfather became terminally ill, then he was in a bed downstairs. We had to take it in turns to sit with him because he couldn't be left alone. One night my older sister, then about 18 years old, was looking after him when suddenly she felt strange and the whole room seemed to go very cold.

She had been sitting at the bottom of the bed and moved towards Grandfather to see if he was alright, but an invisible wall seemed to hold her back. She couldn't get within a couple of feet of him. Then she happened to glance at the fireplace.

On the hearth were two vases and a box of matches. A match had been taken out ready to light a fire and was lying next to the box. However, the whole lot, matches and vases, were not resting on the hearth but hovering in the air about six inches away. My sister gave a great shout for the rest of the family and we all went running into the sick room, and with my own eyes I saw these articles from the hearth hovering in the air.

When my father saw them he rushed forward to grab the articles but as he touched them they fell to the floor. Strangely enough, it wasn't that night my grandfather died, but about three weeks later.

# Shula
## (West Bromwich)

"We have always had a dog or two but my father was particularly fond of one dog, Shula, a black and white mongrel which was mostly terrier. In September 1996 she just keeled over and died.

On the second Wednesday of the following January I was upstairs in my parents' bedroom. When I turned round there was a dog on our bed. I first thought that it was our present dog, a Beagle cross and said, 'What are you doing up here?'. Then I heard my mother talking to our dog downstairs and when I turned round to look at the bed nothing was there. When I thought about it I realised that it had been Shula.

At that time my father seemed well, but the next day at 4.30 in the afternoon, he keeled over and died, in exactly the same way as Shula. I don't know anything about the paranormal, but I often wonder if Shula came to fetch him."

# Coventry

## The Haunted Kitchen
### (Keresley)

When we got married we bought a house in Keresley, near Coventry. We had lived there for a couple of years when my brother in law, who was a builder, came round with a grandiose kitchen extension scheme which took advantage of grants offered at the time. We worked on that kitchen for four or five weeks but it never seemed right. There was something odd about it. It didn't feel normal.

Then strange things begin to happen. I came down one morning to find a pool of water in the middle of the floor. There had been no water there when we went to bed and there were no pipes or water supply anywhere near. I said to my wife, 'Have you spilled anything during the night?' but she hadn't. We just mopped it up and though no more about it.

At 7 o'clock the following morning I came downstairs and suddenly the plastic lid of a margarine box rose into the air in front of me, floated down the kitchen then fell to the floor. 'Am I seeing things here?' I wondered, but I didn't mention it to anyone. That night we had a baby sitter in by the name of Sandra. I asked her if she could make a cup of tea and as she went into the kitchen the kettle flew off the cooker at her.

Once when I came home from work my wife said to me, 'You won't believe this, but you know those new glasses that we bought (we had had a party the previous Saturday), four of them are smashed'. I said, 'Oh no, how did that come about?'. She had washed them, put them on top of the cupboard and they were there for about an hour when they just flew off onto the floor and smashed. This was all happening in the area of the new extension and it was getting out of hand.

There was a bloke at work who was the type who would explain to you all the weird programmes on TV, so I asked him how I could put a stop to it. He told me to get two white candles and place one each end of the kitchen unit as close to six feet apart as I could make it. I didn't have to light them and I didn't need to tell anyone about it, except the wife, of course. He told me to just do it and then forget about them. I said to him, 'I don't believe that that will have any effect' and he replied, 'Well, try it'.

I did as he suggested and, do you know, the strange events stopped. This is a piece of advice which I would like to pass on to anybody else who is having these kind of problems. It worked for me so perhaps it would work for them.

Several years later we came to leave the house, and in the packing and general chaos the candles got moved. All kinds of strange things started happening again. We put the candles back and straight away you could feel a change in the atmosphere.

This guy said that if we moved, the spirits might move with us. We were to leave the candles where they were and if anything strange happened after we moved we were to say, 'I have had enough, I don't want you in my new home'. Anyway, it didn't come with us."

✳✳✳✳✳

Well, if you've got paranormal disturbances, you can try this routine if you like, but don't be surprised if it doesn't work for you. Offhand, we can't think of any reason why it might work and we admit that we've never heard of it before.

It is the case, as doctors know, that if you believe something will work, it often will. Perhaps the bloke at work was practising his own little bit of witchcraft on that basis.

Our two previous books contain other stories about strange happenings following the disturbance of building work. The most spectacular is *The Haunted Shopping Centre* in *Midland Ghosts & Hauntings*. In this book see *Lucy* and *Something Fishy*.

# The Lady on the Stairs
### (Camden, Coventry)

"Not long after my wife and I were married we went to view a house in Camden, Coventry. Having collected the key from the agent we let ourselves in the front door. The house felt colder inside than the out, but I put this down to it not having been lived in for some time. We closed the front door behind us and I went through into the kitchen but my wife stayed by the front door. I started to go up the stairs but then I saw that an "old dear" was coming down, so I pressed myself against the newel post to let her by. I would say that she was in her mid 50s, but I was about 25 at the time and this seemed really ancient. She was quite smart, of average height, and she wore an oldish style coat with the type of fur collar that was popular in the 1920s and 30s. She was also wearing a floppy type of hat which is a female version of the trilby. It was a narrow staircase and I had to lean over the bannister to let her by, but there was still not enough room for both of us so she simply came through me. I didn't feel cold or anything and realised then that she was making absolutely no noise.

45

My wife had gone outside leaving the front door open, and the woman continued down the stairs and out.

I was gobsmacked. I did look around upstairs, and from the clutter and papers it seemed as if someone had left only recently. Closing the door behind me I said to my wife, 'I'm not going in there again.' ."

# Kid and
# the Lemon Grass
## (Coventry)

"My husband died at a quarter to 12 one night in 1975. We had two daughters, the older one was living with us, but the younger whom my husband used to call 'Kid', was living away from home. My older daughter and I decided we wouldn't ring Kid at that time of the night to tell her the news but wait until the morning. The next morning we telephoned and she said, 'It's alright, I know Father has died, he died at a quarter to 12'. We asked how she knew and her reply was, 'He came and said goodbye to me'. Her telephone had rung at a quarter to 12 and when she picked it up a disembodied voice had said, 'Well, cheerio Kid', then the line went dead. There had been no sound of a disconnection, nothing.

My husband was very fond of lemon grass soap and he would use it all the time so that the whole house reeked of it. After he died I would quite often come home and smell this soap. I thought it was just my imagination until the day that I brought a friend home and she said, 'What's that lovely smell?'.

✶✶✶✶✶

Yet another aroma to add to the catalogue. They are usually flowers or tobacco and quite pleasant, but see *Something Fishy*, about the unfortunate lady from Aston. Here you will also find references to other cases.

# Shropshire

## Romans in the Garden
### (Dorrington)

"I have lived here ever since the house was built 40 years ago. We keep a guest house and, of course, I sometimes have to get up very early in the morning to prepare breakfast. In early April of 1995 I got up at about 4.30 when it was only half light and I happened to look out of the bedroom window. We have a large lawn set with chairs, tables and umbrellas and there, to my surprise, I saw about five people sitting around a table. I thought, 'Oh dear me, some of the guests have got up early. I had better hurry up with the breakfasts'.

Then I took another look and thought, 'Those aren't guests.'. They looked like Roman soldiers, with helmets, shields and everything, and they were deep in conversation, chatting away. There they were, these very ancient people lounging around on my modern garden furniture.

I told my wife but all she said was, 'Come back to bed.'. Just then the telephone rang and I had to run downstairs. After that I started preparing breakfast and that was the end of the story as far as I was concerned. It would have gone out of my mind completely and I would have put it down to imagination or something, were it not for something that happened six months later.

By this time it would have been getting into the autumn. It was a cold night when not a lot of people were about, and I was starting to lock up and put out the lights at about 10.30 when my wife told me we still had a couple of late arriving guests to come.

I sat in the lounge waiting until they came at about 11 o clock. We went through the formalities, then the woman guest said to me, 'What are all those people doing in your drive? Is it a fancy dress party?'. She said that they were standing around the drive and the lawn, and that they all seemed to be dressed as Roman soldiers. Then she described exactly what I had seen six months earlier. I didn't know her at all and I hadn't seen her before or since.

I didn't mention my experience because I was more interested in getting information about what she had seen. She just thought that a party was going on and saw nothing spooky in it at all.

We are about 7 miles south west of Wroxeter which was the third largest Roman city in Great Britain. Part of the Roman road known as Watling Street ran from Leintwardine to Church Stretton and passes near Wroxeter. Several little roads branched off it and one runs through our grounds, you can see the marks."

✱✱✱✱✱

In *Midland Spirits & Spectres* we published another Roman ghost story – see *Roman Horses*, when two metal detector enthusiasts were working overnight in a field near Telford. Some readers may have heard the well known story about the cellar in York which is sometimes marched through by a troop of Roman soldiers. There is also a legion which tramps by night through part of Hampshire. There may be no more Roman ghosts than any other variety, but their dress and equipment makes them more obviously similar than black monks or grey ladies.

The interaction between Roman legionnaires and modern garden furniture makes you wonder if the visitors knew what they were sitting on and what they might have made of it. In facts it presents the question – do these apparitions think and have consciousness?

# The Linesman
## (Severn Valley Railway)

"I am a steam railway enthusiast and a volunteer for the Severn Valley Railway.

One afternoon, in the middle of the summer of 1987 about eight of us were testing the line at Bridgnorth. We were nearing the Knowlesands tunnel when we saw, about 15 yards ahead, a man walking away from us towards the tunnel. He was quite ordinary looking, of average height and middle aged. It was obvious that he was a permanent way man whose job it is to test the line because he was carrying a key hammer and a fishplate spanner. We were a bit suspicious because he wasn't wearing a high visibility vest.

Three of us were slightly ahead of the other five. We turned round to say that somebody else was on the line, but when we looked back he had disappeared. I heard later that in 1896, a permanent way man had been killed in the tunnel, so perhaps it was him."

# Little Girl Humming
## (Little Dawley, Telford)

"Strange things have been going on in this block of terraced houses for a long time. Although I've only lived here for a few years, I am next door to my husband's family and I've heard about the earlier goings on from my sister in law, Tracey*.

My mother in law said that, in her house, someone was following her around. They have heard footsteps and seen doors mysteriously open and close. On one occasion, Tracey was looking for something and when her mother heard a deep sighing from the bottom of the stairs, she thought it was because Tracey couldn't find what she wanted. She called out 'Haven't you found it yet?'. There was no reply, so she opened the door and was surprised to find that Tracey was still upstairs. The sighing noise at the bottom of the stairs has been heard several times.

Tracey is now 20 and she has told me, in confidence, that when she was about 10 or 11 she saw the apparition of a little girl at the bottom of the stairs. She was wearing a purple top with a V-neck and had long fair hair. Tracey wasn't frightened or anything, she just went off to bed.

When we moved into our house nothing happened for a good 18 months. Then I began to feel that someone was watching me. One night, after my husband had gone to work I was ironing and I went into the kitchen. The kitchen door and the front door are in line, and each has a pane of clear glass. Through the glass of the front door I could just see a little girl of 12 or 15, no older than 16.

In the 1970's my mum used to do my hair by taking the side bits up to tie on top and leaving the rest down, so that I had long hair at the back. This little girl had her fair hair in a style just like that. She was wearing a purple top with a V-neck and pointed collar, of the type that you saw in the 70's. Although she was standing there and I could see her clearly, I could actually see through her, as if she were a reflection. She was there for ten or fifteen minutes. I had this feeling that I must not turn round and I was really frightened. I don't think she was there to hurt me and I have never felt threatened, it was just fear of the unknown. I mentioned none of this to my children because I didn't want them to get alarmed.

On another evening I was in the bath reading a book, my husband was downstairs and the children were in bed, when suddenly I heard someone humming that Brahms lullaby, *'Slumber sweetly my love'*. It was a young female voice. I jumped out of the bath and hastily rubbed myself down, but as soon as I got out of the water the singing stopped. It was coming from the room next to the bathroom, which was empty. I looked in all the children's bedrooms but they were fast asleep. I said to my husband, 'Did you hear anything?', but he hadn't, in any case he was downstairs. I know I didn't imagine it, it was too clear. I'm certain that I distinctly heard somebody humming. It was really weird."

# Staffordshire

## Ghosts on the Canals
### (Kinver)

Job Clarke is named after his grandfather who worked a canal boat for the Shropshire Union Railways & Canal Company. It was taken over by London & North Western Railway in 1922 and became part of the London, Midland and Scottish in 1923.

"Every time I see an old boat my heart beats faster, there's something about them. My grandfather and grandmother lived on the boats. I have heard that they had sixteen children but only six lived. Grandmother was 87 when she died after working on the boats all her life and loving every minute. My father was the youngest of the family and one of his brothers (my uncle) was also named Job Clarke. Grandfather's boat was the *Idris* and my uncles had the *Antwerp* and the *Saturn*.

My mother often talked about Ellesmere Port on the River Mersey which is at the end of the Shropshire Union Canal, so one day I decided to visit the Boat Museum there. I told some of the staff about the different boats and mentioned the Saturn. They said 'We've got it here. It arrived yesterday.' The museum said that the Saturn was the only surviving flyboat. I doubt that because flyboats were built to move fast and were kept very clean and not knocked about like the other boats.

About fifty years ago, when I was 14, I had to take a horse along the towpath to meet my uncle who was waiting on a boat at Kinver on the Staffordshire and Worcestershire Canal. It was starting to get dark as I came to a bridge near the village where the towpath runs under the bridge and a road runs over the top. Just past the bridge was a field and I knew that the ground by the towpath was very marshy and impossible for anyone to cross. However, standing there, where no animal could stand, was a dark horse with a rider. The horse was standing still but moved its head slightly. I saw it plain as day and I saw the animal's reflection on the canal. Then I noticed that the horse had an old fashioned barbed bit, that is, with a long curve coming out of the mouth with a chain on it. Barbed bits are still used but now they're much shorter and the old fashioned type hadn't been used for years. That did frighten me. I was afraid to walk past and stopped there for half a minute wondering what to do. My fright spooked my horse and she bolted.

Later, I told my dad and he said, 'You're a liar'. I told other people and no doubt they thought the same.

Some ten years later I read in the *Kidderminster Shuttle* newspaper that a woman walking over the bridge late at night with a pram saw the same thing, a rider out on that very marshy ground. She called the police who came out with dogs but they found nothing.

About two years after that I was talking to a chap who said that the area was called Gibbet Lane, where people were hung. I didn't know anything about that until he told me.

*The wheel works at Cookley on the Staffordshire & Worcestershire Canal.*

When I was about 11 years old [1947] I started off with my two uncles to take a boat from Stourport up the Staffordshire & Worcestershire Canal to Wolverhampton. The horse was fresh to the job and needed to be led, so one uncle led the horse while the other went ahead to open the locks and I had to steer the boat.

Imagine the situation. It was so foggy that I couldn't even see the cabin from 6 feet away. The boat was 70 feet long so there was no way I could see the front of it, though I could just see the sparks from the horse's hooves. To make matter worse, there are eighteen locks on the Staffs & Worcs, then twenty one more up the rise into the centre of Wolverhampton which will take you two and a half hours.

The Staffordshire & Worcestershire canal runs through the western suburbs of Wolverhampton where it is met at Aldersley Junction by the Birmingham Canal. To join this and get to the middle of Wolverhampton you have to make a sharp right turn, almost a hairpin bend. You have to unfasten the line from the horse to the boat, lead the horse over a bridge to the other side of the canal, steer the boat round and retie the line. The average person would find it difficult to manoeuvre the bend in broad daylight with a mate, but I had to do it single handed in thick fog.

I got completely lost. I was terrified. I sat there for a minute, thinking 'What can I do?', then I heard a voice in my head telling me to follow the line. It seemed to tell me where to go, saying 'In a bit, out a bit', and so on. I would feel a slight bump as the boat slid perfectly into the locks.

When I got to Wolverhampton all the fog lights were on. We tied up and went to bed. The next morning we met my cousin and various friends, and my cousin complained that the boats had been bumping and banging all night. Then he said to my uncle, 'I didn't hear you come in, you were very quiet, who was steering the boat?'. I told him that I did, single handed. He and his fellow boatmen said that there had been only one person who could steer a boat single handed through those locks in a fog and that was my grandad, Job Clarke.

I never found out why my uncles never stopped to see if I was alright. From that day on they never brought the subject up."

# Uncle Dave's Watchchain
## (Stafford)

"Several years ago I was sitting downstairs in the lounge with my mother and my sister. My niece aged 7 had gone to bed, but she suddenly appeared in the doorway and said to her mother, 'There is a gentleman standing by my bed and he won't go away', and she described him.

He was not very tall, he wore a gold watch chain hanging in two loops with a red stone attached, and he had a horrible hole in the side of his face. When she had been settled in bed again, my mother said, 'You know who she's describing don't you, it's Uncle Dave'. Dave always wore a gold watch chain in a double loop and the chain had a red garnet in it. He suffered from a disease commonly known as The King's Evil which disfigured the side of his face. Mother had never seen him.

Later we heard that Uncle Dave died that night".

#### ✱✱✱✱✱

The Kings Evil was scrofula, a tubercular infection of the neck and throat. It was supposed to be cured only by a touch from the King of England.

# Go Home Jack
## (Wednesfield)

Harry Onions told us about some unusual features of his new home.

"Me and my wife recently moved into this little bungalow. After we have had our meal at night we lock the back door and go into the living room to watch telly. While we were sitting we often heard the back door shut although it had already been locked. Then when we went to bed at 11 o'clock we might hear the bedroom door shutting, though it was already closed. Sometimes we could feel somebody moving round the bed and leaning on it. One particular night I could feel that something was there in the room, then suddenly the clothes were dragged off the bed and I was left lying there with nothing on. Me and the wife are not frightened of ghosts but I was a bit put out.

Our son lives in London with his girlfriend and because we had not long moved he had never had the chance to visit us. His girlfriend had never been to this part of the country. One day my son phoned me to say that his girlfriend had something to tell me. He put her on the phone and she said, 'I have a vision of two bungalows together', which was right, and then she surprised me. She gave me the name of the man who lived here before us and told me some facts about him, and she also told me what to do. I was to get two saucepan lids, go into the corner of each room and make a noise, and as I went round I was to call out, 'Jack - go home!'. I said, 'If I do that you'll have me missus putting me away'.

I'm a caller at our local bingo session and I happened to say to the vicar, 'What would you say if I told you I have a ghost?'. The vicar said that I would have to go and see a ghost buster. I told him, 'I'm serious', and he said he would come round the next morning. When he came he said a little prayer and then he got a bottle of holy water and started sprinkling it about. Since then we haven't had a problem. He gave me some holy water that was left over but we haven't heard the ghost since.

The vicar said that 95% of the time this will work but in the other 5% he has to go back a second time. He did say that the ghost was a gentleman who lived here with his sister. When he died, apparently, his sister arranged a big party at a nearby pub, but just as they were carrying his coffin out to the funeral his sister dropped dead in the bathroom. The vicar said that the reason he was still about was that he was trying to find his sister. Evidently the vicar told him to go home and rest, and that his sister didn't live here any more."

# Simon
## (Stoke on Trent)

"I have still got my dog. He died about ten years ago but last year he came back. For some days I had heard a scratching noise in the skirting board and thought I had a mouse, but it turned out to be the pattering of paws and it was my old dog, a Dachshund called Simon. He was 15 years old when I lost him. He's in my house nearly all the time, doing all the things he used to do when he was alive. About 9 o'clock most nights I feel him get up on the settee and push his way round the back of me. He lies on the cushion at the back of my neck and I can't move for him. He's in bed every night, most probably he's there now while I'm on the phone. He likes to snuggle down in the back of my knees. Usually I can only feel and hear him, but I have seen him about four times. Once he was by my electric fire and once at the bottom of my bed just about to jump onto the floor. Another time he was asleep just a few feet away. As soon as he knows that I have seen him he goes.

I have tried to touch him but he disappears so quickly. However, I did manage to touch him once. I could only see half of him but I could make out that he was lying on his back. He looked as if he was dead and when I touched him he was stone cold. I was scared then."

# Black Bob, the Dark Lady and the Colonel
## (Tettenhall)

Tettenhall was a Staffordshire village in 1776 when a school was established with strong links to the Church of England. Nearly a century later, in 1863, the Baptists and Congregationalists bought an old house, now occupied by the headmaster, converted it into Tettenhall College and opened it with fifteen boys. The first headmaster was the Reverend Robert Halley, commonly known as Black Bob.

At the beginning of each New Year he would march his pupils to Albrighton where each new pupil was held by the ankles and lowered down until his face touched the water of a lake near the church. After that it was to the local shop for fizzy pop and bull's eyes. Strange to say, the boys did not seem to object and the College more than doubled in size during the first year. At the beginning of the 20th century and for several decades, the ghost of Black Bob appeared regularly at Tettenhall College. Local people say that he walked round the grounds checking his wells.

A dark lady is also said to walk the buildings. The door to the cold room in the cellar is high up and to reach it you have to climb a flight of little steps. Once or twice a term the college chef, a solid, well built man from West Bromwich, sees something out of the corner of his eye:

"The first time I caught sight of the legs disappearing up the flight of steps I thought somebody was there. I put down what I was doing and went to see who it was. I would say that the legs belong to an elderly woman, they have black lace up boots and a black flowing skirt down to the ankle."

Rumour has it that the dark lady was a servant who threw herself from the balcony in the 1870's, but there is no evidence for this.

Sometimes the organ in the College chapel can be heard playing when no one is there. Alex Poile, the groundsman, has heard it. Tettenhall Towers is now part of the College and Alex also has a story to tell about its builder.

"Colonel Thorneycroft was born in Willenhall in 1822, the son of an ironmaster. After the death of his father the Colonel ran the family iron works for 26 years, during which time he bought or leased large areas of land so that he became an important landowner. He was a magistrate in Wolverhampton and Shropshire, High Sheriff of Staffordshire and Deputy Lord Lieutenant.

He purchased a wayside inn and converted it into his splendid residence, Tettenhall Towers. He built the Victorian Gothic towers and a private theatre which may still be the biggest of its kind in the country. Among its Heath Robinson type embellishments were a sprung floor, a device for blowing real fire up the chimney, a 40 foot high water cascade and a wind machine with hot, cold or scented air. The Colonel and his family took part in shows, usually to raise money for charity.

The Colonel spent much of his time inventing various devices. After a hair raising ride in a balloon which slowly drifted close to some blast furnaces, he came up with an idea for steering a balloon. It is said that he invented wings and persuaded a butler to jump from the top of the tower wearing them. The butler landed unhurt in a rhododendron bush. This was a little out of character because the Colonel usually treated his staff well. Often, when he and his grooms had been out for the day, he would take them to a pub, order them half a gallon of beer and leave them to it while he took the carriage home. Before he died he sold Tettenhall Towers to the college.

To return to Alex Poile's story: "At 11 am on the Sunday morning of the last weekend in October 1986, two electricians from Stuart Aulton Electrical Contractors of Wolverhampton were here, both down to earth Black Country lads. They were working in our theatre, which is still intact but the ornamentation has gone. They were in a dark corner of the stage putting in smoke detectors and checking the wiring. One of them was up the ladder and the other was holding it. Suddenly, the overhead lighting went very dim. They tried the switch but it stayed dim. After playing around with the lights Stuart said, 'Don't worry, we've nearly finished anyway'.

The chap holding the ladder had had no previous experience of ghosts but suddenly he said, 'It's gone very cold, this is spooky'. Then he added, 'I think we're being watched'. Stuart turned round and said, 'Oh my God.'

A man was floating in the air watching them very sternly. He had a walrus moustache and a black Victorian jacket, which sounds very like Colonel Thorneycroft. He floated across the stage, through a black curtain and then through a solid wall at the back of the theatre, in all for about 10 seconds. Both electricians left the building abandoning all their equipment.

The man at the bottom of the ladder has now refused to work anywhere in the place. I don't know whether they saw a ghost or not but they definitely saw something. Stuart came back to finish the job but he brought his wife and a radio and he keeps looking over his shoulder now."

# The Haunted Castle
## (Tamworth Castle)

In 770 the Anglo Saxon king, Offa, built a fortress at Tamworth which became a stronghold of the kings of Mercia. It was destroyed by invading Vikings but rebuilt in 913 by a great warrior queen, Ethelfleda.

After the Norman invasion of 1066 William the Conqueror gave the castle and its lands to the Marmion family. By the third generation the estate had passed into the hands of Robert Marmion, a warlike and quarrelsome character.

A convent at nearby Polesworth belonged to the castle. It had been founded in 827 by Egbert of Wessex and his daughter or grand daughter, later Saint Editha, became the first Abbess. The acquisitive Baron Marmion evicted the nuns from their home so that they had to take sanctuary at Oldbury, near Nuneaton. So much is historical fact, and from that the legends grew.

Saint Editha, it seems, was so annoyed by the eviction that one night in 1139 she rose from her tomb and appeared to Robert Marmion. Unless he returned the nuns to Polesworth Abbey, she told him, he should 'suffer an evil death and go to hell'. Marmion was not impressed, so to show that she meant business saintly Editha 'smote him with her crozier' on the side of his head.

There are various accounts of the after effects. Some say there was a terrible flow of blood, others refer to a nasty pain and there is also a story of a wound which would not heal. However, they all agree that Marmion recognised that to get rid of his disability he had to find a priest and vow to restore the nuns to Polesworth Abbey. As soon as Marmion took the vow, of course, he was well again.

A room in the old part of the tower is thought to have been Robert Marmion's bedroom. So many people have reported seeing the ghost of a lady in black, presumed to be a nun, in the room and nearby, that it is known as the haunted room.

*The Castle pictured in the early 1700s and now. Sorry about the scaffolding. Look carefully and you will see that the only difference is that the Flemish gabled bits on the left have gone.*

There is also a lady in white who is often seen on or near the battlements. She is thought by some people to be linked with mural paintings which once adorned the walls of the banqueting hall. They showed a battle in which a knight, Sir Tarquin, was killed in the Lady Meadow below the battlements by one Lancelot du Lac. The white lady is said to be Tarquin's mistress who was watching from the battlements. She was betrothed to another knight and so had to grieve in silence, so her unhappy spirit will not rest and wanders about the walls. It is almost a shame to reveal that Lancelot du Lac is an invention of medieval French storytellers.

Hearing these ghostly legends, the then Assistant Curator and four other men, one of them a photographer, decided to spend the night of 22nd October 1949 in the castle. At the bottom of a staircase which leads from Robert Marmion's bedroom they set up their equipment and sealed off both the stairs and the bedroom by tying string across and sealing it.

Strange things happened throughout the night. At 7 minutes past 12 they heard a door to the room above being pushed gently open and soft footsteps walking from it. When they began coming down the stairs towards the group of watchers the photographer shouted, 'I'm going to take a picture.'. A developed photograph showed a strange shadow vaguely the shape of a human head. The Assistant Curator concluded his account of the night's events by saying, 'Until this experience I was completely doubtful of the existence of supernatural agencies, but I am no longer of that opinion'.

Fifteen years later (1964) the then Custodian, Norman Seckington, found his pet spaniel whining at the door to the Warder's Lodge. He let the dog in, but it took one look inside the Lodge and shot out with wild eyes and bristling hair. It bolted through the courtyard and was never seen again.

On 28 July 1965 another group of ghost hunters locked themselves in the castle with both camera and tape recorder. They heard footsteps, feminine sighs and a final moan, which were all captured on tape.

In 2000 we visited Tamworth Castle and spoke to some of the staff. Museum Attendant Barbara Adams remembers a time when the present shop was a store room. She and the Senior Museum Attendant went into the room and both felt as if they were being crushed. She said it was quite frightening. Barbara also remembers the security video system being installed.

'A white shadow floated across the hall, hovered, then shot away in a different direction. It was picked up by the cameras and lasted for about 10 or 15 minutes. Two of us went to investigate and we couldn't see anything but we felt cold.'

The equipment was checked and rechecked but no explanation was ever found.

Barbara's colleague, David Nickells, once sensed the ghost on the stairs with him.

'I ran up one of the staircases and felt something running with me. I have always been sceptical but it's in the back of my mind about the place being haunted. I would say there's something here.'

Val Lee has worked at the Castle since 1984 and has heard all kind of strange tales but she has had only one alarming experience.

'I was locking up one dark winter evening and as I climbed the tower stairs the door at the bottom slammed shut behind me. I continued up the stairs, locked up, went down again and found that I couldn't open the door. Fortunately I had my radio and I was able to call somebody to let me out. At first I thought somebody had been playing a joke but nobody was around at that time. The little hook which goes across the door had fastened itself on the other side. That was a bit frightening. Fortunately, it only happened once.'

June Hall tells a most unusual story.

'We hear footsteps coming from empty rooms now and again and also voices. We can hear a man's voice and muffled conversation, nothing distinct. It seems to come mostly from the south side, which is the newer part.

I particularly remember one incident which occurred in 1998, I think in April. It was about a quarter to 9 in the morning and my colleague and I were going to open up the north side of the building. We went upstairs into what is now the Tamworth Story room. It used to be the Long Gallery and was probably bedrooms in the 17<sup>th</sup> century.

I was halfway across the room with my colleague a few yards behind when suddenly it felt as if sand had been thrown in my face. It made me shut my eyes. I looked down at the floor, expecting to see sand or some kind of granule, but there was nothing. When I looked up again I could see a thick blue cloud, about two feet across but not deep. It looked as if someone had taken a puff of a cigar then walked out of the room, though of course this was not the case because we were the only ones in the building.

By this time my colleague had caught up with me and asked, 'What's the matter?', because I was just standing there. I said, 'I have just had something thrown into my face' and asked her if she could see the blue smoke. She said, 'Oh yes'. The blue cloud moved quite quickly towards the window on my left, then it suddenly disappeared. I was very glad that she saw it too, or I might have thought I had run up the stairs too quickly or something and was having a funny turn.'

Ann Williams was Shop Supervisor and as such she put in a long working week. Besides running the shop she helped with general managerial work such as organising visiting parties

'There were a lot of strange things happening in the Castle. We often had children here and they would say things like, 'Why was the lady crying?', or, 'Who was that funny little man?'. They seemed to be very sensitive.

When we had evening visitors there were always two members of staff present. Just before they arrived I would stand behind the reception desk and take their money. Often we heard footsteps coming from the castle when all the visitors were in front of us in the reception area. Then we would look at each other and say, 'They're at it again!'.

We were having our break when a really funny incident occurred. The lids of coffee jars are screwed on quite tightly, but with my own eyes I saw the lid on our jar unscrew by itself and flip off the jar. My colleague said calmly, 'Oh, it's OK, you can make yourself a cup of coffee if you wish'.

There is a particular room where anyone entering triggers a sensor and a flute begins to play. If I stand there for long I feel someone running their fingers down my back. Sometimes I would sit doing my paperwork and I knew that somebody else was there. I didn't feel threatened, it's just that somebody was there.

I was used to all this and normally it did not affect me, but on the evening of 24th February 1999 I was really scared. The alarms had sounded and I was called out by the police because I was a key holder. It was pitch dark, rain was lashing down and a storm blowing. Nothing was wrong but an engineer was called out to reset the system, so I waited inside the castle for him to arrive. It was 1.30 am and I was alone in the semi darkness of the reception area.

Above me was the curator's office. First I began to hear the odd footstep but the sounds rapidly became louder and more frequent until it sounded as if a party were taking place overhead. I could hear a murmur of voices and a stamping of feet as if there was a crowd up there.

The Curator had just bought a new beech table and the resident ghost didn't seem to like it because I heard him dragging it across the floor. We quite agree with the ghost. The new table was in light wood while all the other pieces of furniture are lovely, dark antiques, so it didn't fit at all. That night I heard this dragging noise loudly and distinctly.

Suddenly I felt overcome by an overwhelming presence. For the first time ever I felt as if I wasn't supposed to be there. I went numb with fright and had such an intense feeling that other people were there that I had to get out.

It was too cold to go outside so I stood in the porch. Next to me, just inside the front door, was the telephone. When it rang I jumped, but it was only the engineer telling me that he had arrived and was waiting for me outside the front door.

I was just inside and he was just outside. I pulled the door open and he said, 'Good grief, it didn't take you long to run down. I saw you looking out for me'. I told him I hadn't been upstairs. He replied that he definitely saw a figure looking out of the window which seemed to be a woman. He saw her from the top of a slope above the castle but as he got nearer she walked away. I asked him which window and he pointed to the Ferrer's Room, which is the Curator's office.'

Many people have had strange experiences at Tamworth Castle but an actual sighting of a ghost is very rare. However, this happened to Sue Fudge, who has been a Museum Attendant since about 1989.

'This place is not frightening at all. It has a nice atmosphere and is very pleasant to work in. I have only had the one experience. In fact, I was beginning to think that nothing every happened to me and I wasn't at all psychic or whatever.

On Sundays we don't open until 2 o'clock, so we get there at about 1.30 pm. The curtains are closed when we go off duty each evening, so when we arrive our first job is to open them again. First we open the curtains to the breakfast parlour curtains, then we walk through a connecting door to the drawing room.

I was standing behind a green leather sofa which came from Drayton Manor and once belonged to Sir Robert Peel [1788 -1850], MP for Tamworth, Prime Minister and founder of the police force] when suddenly, I noticed that there was a lady sitting in the corner of the sofa.

The sofa is deep and she must have been quite a small person; I could only see her head and shoulders. She looked about 40 years old and was wearing a blue dress. She had a nice, pleasant face, quite pale and ordinary. Her hair was dark and she wore something white on her head, a bit of lace or something.

Victorian women could wear their hair long before they were married but afterwards they had to wear it up and would put a lace cap on top. She didn't seem to have long hair so it must have been piled up on top. She turned, looked at me and smiled. The next second I blinked and she was gone.

People have asked me if she could have been one of the Victorian family who used to live here, but I saw her for only a second so I couldn't really say. I wasn't upset by the ghost; what was really unsettling was a negative feeling which I have never experienced before or since. When the castle closed that day I said to my colleagues that I must go back and close those curtains, because if I didn't do it then I would never go back in the that room.'

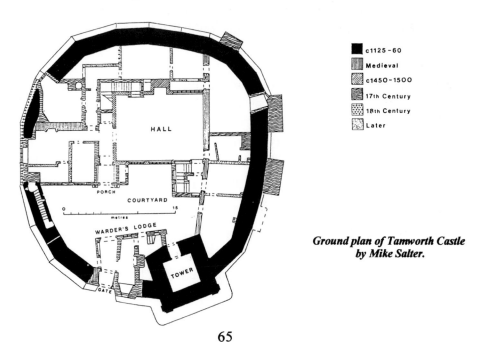

*Ground plan of Tamworth Castle by Mike Salter.*

# Warwickshire

## The Phantom Coach
### (Coughton Court)

The young businessman who saw this apparition now lives in Stratford upon Avon.

"This is the only ghostly experience I have ever had. It must have been about 1993 or 1994. My wife and I had been to the UCI cinema at Shirley and it was nearly midnight when I was driving back home to Alcester along the old Roman road, the A435.

It was a quiet night, very, very dark with no moon. My wife was dozing in the car. Just as I drove down into Coughton I had a sensation of something strange and this white light appeared. It all happened in a flash but I'm sure that I saw, for a split second, an old fashioned carriage. It came out from a gap between the houses just before you get to Sambourne Lane and crossed the road from right to left. Then it drove across the grass straight towards the main door of the Court, but not down the drive. It wasn't ten or fifteen metres away and coming out in front of my car it made me swerve to the left. It was very bright in a whitish haze, almost like the ghosts you see on a horror film. I didn't see any horses but I saw a larger wheel at the back of the carriage and a smaller at the front, and on top, sitting up high, I saw the lower part of a man's body. He was wearing straight, tight fitting boots which finished just below the knee."

His wife says that he woke her up with a loud profanity followed by 'Did you see that?!'

"I couldn't believe what I was seeing. I don't believe in things like that but for a moment I experienced total fear. The hair stood up on the back of my neck and my arms were all goose pimples. It wasn't logical and you didn't expect to see it.

Afterwards, thinking back, you tend to trivialise such an experience. You think, I didn't really see that, I must have seen something else, and you try to think of a logical explanation. We hadn't been to see a horror film or anything like that. It was almost like the headlights of a car, but it couldn't have been a car, I could make out the wheels and the boots. Was it flashing headlights or a torch? Nothing I have ever seen creates that kind of light.

The next time I drove down there I was very wary in case there was a repeat performance."

# Past Residents
## (A village near Stratford on Avon)

"I'm almost frightened to tell it. I don't even sleep in the room where it happened and I really don't like talking about it. It hasn't only been me. There has been a ghost in the village and other people have had strange experiences. Many people say that they have been walking along when someone touched them. One little girl used to talk to the ghost of an elderly man and her mother had the vicar in to bless the house.

The village church was built in the 12th century and our cottage goes back to the 17th, or possibly the 15th century. I've never had time to research its history. I have been told that the part of the house where all this happened was once used for bible lessons.

The events began when we made some major alterations to the house involving moving stairs and building an extension. My baby son had always slept reasonably well, but as soon as we put his cot where the stairs had been he woke up night after night. One of my little girls said that an old lady walked down the stairs with her. Sometimes, out of the corner of my eye, I see something moving through the hall, but when I look nobody is there.

A dear old man who had recently lost his wife lived opposite so I kept an eye on him. I'm quite good with old people. Then he had to go into hospital, where he died. The next night a man's voice woke me saying, 'Come on! Come on!'. I came to thinking it was one of my children, but it wasn't. Standing at the bottom of my bed was the figure of an old lady. Although it was very clear I can't remember the details of what she was wearing. I didn't write anything down at the time and I've done my best to forget it. She was small, she wore a bonnet and had a shawl over her head in an old burgundy colour. The unusual thing was that she glowed with a warm light. She was smiling, so I know that she was being kind, but I was just frightened of the unknown. I tugged on the light cord in the ceiling so hard that I pulled it out.

After that I didn't want to go to bed at night. Everybody says to me it must have been a dream, but I know that it wasn't, I know the old woman was there, it was so real. At the time I thought she might be the wife of the old man who had come back to thank me for looking after him, but her clothes were much older than that. I have asked the neighbours who lived in the house in the past, but none of the occupiers within living memory answer the description of the old lady.

She is not our only ghost. We had a friend, a lonely chap who used to come here often and became almost part of the family. He used to smoke and when he died, we began to smell tobacco in the house. I can often smell it, my husband can only smell it occasionally when he says something like, 'You should come into the lounge, your friend's tobacco is really strong there.'.

It's taken me two years to get over that first experience. It really frightened me. I certainly wouldn't mess about with a Ouija board or anything like that."

# Lucy
## (Henley in Arden)

"I'm a sceptic really and I don't believe in ghosts as such. I do believe in spirits but not the kind that materialise.

I lived in a beautiful old black and white house in Henley in Arden. We moved there during World War II and remained for about forty years, raising three children. Our bedroom was on the back staircase which was quite winding. Every time I went to the landing outside that room I had an eerie feeling, as if someone was watching me. When I went upstairs I liked to go with someone.

We had a near hurricane in Henley which blew down one of our chimneys so that it fell through our bedroom ceiling. We moved temporarily to another room, but on our first night I woke up and screamed. We were in a double bed, my husband was awake and he said, 'Don't worry, I can feel it too'. I couldn't feel anything but I could see the impression of a woman in Elizabethan type costume standing at the far side of the bed and leaning over my husband. By the time I had woken up properly, seen the apparition and screamed, it had vanished. Each of our three children had a room of their own and I kept their doors and mine open during the night. I said to my husband, 'Shut the door.'. My husband said, 'But what if one of the children should wake up?' I said, 'Damn the children, I'm frightened'.

We had a panelled drawing room and there were mice behind the panelling. Several years later I got fed up with the mice and had it removed, but when the builders came to do the work they found an unusual type of wall behind. It wasn't daub and wattle but more like a sack cloth. There had been a story that years ago a girl had been walled up in there. I don't know if this had anything to do with it, but when the work was finished the eerie feeling went and the house had a nice atmosphere.

During the late 1960's we wanted to convert the outhouses into living accommodation, but since it was listed property we had to advertise and put up a notice to see if anyone had anything to say about it.

I had a letter from a lady somewhere the other side of Birmingham saying that she had been a chambermaid there when she was 21. She wrote about this and that, then she wanted to know if anyone had ever seen Lucy, the ghost. She described the landing around my bedroom and even drew a little sketch. Every night she would get her cocoa from the kitchen and take it up the back stairs to the servant's quarters on the third floor, but on the first floor she would meet Lucy and talk to her.

I phoned the writer and we talked for a long time. I invited her to visit, but she never came. She was very old so I assume she has died."

# A Wizened Old Face
## (Portway)

"In 1997 we had a caravan at Wixford and we would go there at weekends. At about 9.30 one Sunday evening towards the end of the summer we were driving home along the straight road from Evesham to Beckett's Farm (the old Alcester road) when it was just going into darkness. My husband was driving and we had just reached the bridge immediately before the turn off to the Portway, when a black face with a hood jumped on to our windscreen. It was definitely not a black plastic bag or anything like that. We saw it clearly and it was a horrible, ugly, wizened old face with a hood, but just a head and shoulders with no body.

It landed on my husband's side of the windscreen. He leaned right over towards me to try and get away from it. I said, 'Keep driving, keep driving. It could have caused us to have a really bad accident. Then it slithered over to my side and looked at me through the windscreen and straight into my eyes, as if it was trying to find out what I really did look like. It frightened me so much that I leaned right back, pressing hard against the seat to try and get away from it. It really unnerved us.

Nobody else saw it and there wasn't another car in sight, it was very quiet and eerie. A few week's later on the breakfast programme, Judy and Richard told a story of something similar which had happened in another part of the country."

# The Haunted School
## (Mysteryville)

Cynthia* worked in a private boarding school which had been established before World War II in a large and ancient house. It is still running so we have disguised its location and identity.

"I gathered a lot of stories over the four years or so I worked there. One, which I think is confused with another stately home, is about a curate falling downstairs and killing himself, but I'm very sceptical about that story.

We met the ghost on one or two occasions, a very benign presence, no one felt frightened at all. It cooks things. We never saw it but we met the results of its culinary efforts. We could tell that it was about by the smell of rice pudding, roast meat, toast, cocoa. There were no kitchens on the premises because they had been removed some years previously.

The smells were outside my office and across the corridor where Matron had her offices, which were on two floors. Later on I had the very good fortune to be given copies of some of the early plans for the house covering the cellars and the main floor. We discovered that in times gone by my room had been the dining room and below me had been the kitchen. The matron's rooms had been the servants' quarters and the two had been linked together.

Matron was more sensitive to the ghostly goings on than any of us and said that in the early days of the school she had encountered it many times. Things happened in her office which didn't happen anywhere else, for example, pictures falling off the wall and papers shuffled about during the night. One night, not long after we first moved in, she was kneeling on the floor working on some papers when she felt a rush of cold wind. Her office was on two floors and as soon as she had a door put in on the second floor, these events largely ceased. She could still smell cooking and strange things still happened in her office, but much less often, and she never felt the rush of cold air again.

A previous school caretaker had been in charge of a contact alarm system. He had lived in a suite at the school and was forever having to get up at night to deal with ringing alarms. He would get up and find doors open that he knew he had closed. In the end they had to dispense with the system.

Some workmen came to carry out work in the cellar and said that they had felt a presence there. Not long before I left some major construction work was in hand and the builders took over the space downstairs and the servants' hall. I didn't usually mention the presence because some people are very sensitive about this kind of thing, but one day I was teasing one of the chaps and asked if he had come across the ghost. I explained that he would smell things. He replied 'Bacon and eggs?'. I nodded and he said, 'We have already met.'

There was a unusual incident during the time when that work was going on. Matron and I were standing in the entrance hall when we both smelt candlewax. We had no candles, there was no need of them.

With this ghost there was nothing dramatic or frightening, just a series of small events. Sometimes it amused us, sometimes we felt that it was an oddity. We never got any closer to solving the riddle of who or what it was. I left the school a little time ago and no doubt there have been many more incidents.

The ghost was rather delightful. The house is very beautiful and it deserves an historic caretaker."

# The White Angel
## (Stratford upon Avon)

"During World War II I was a child and my much older sister was a nurse. We shared a bed and she often woke me up when she came late to bed. She was a nervous type and I used to lie in the pitch black, waiting until she had laid her clothes on the dressing table, then I would jump out on her. I did it often but she still screamed.

One night I was lying there waiting for the right moment to jump, when I saw a shape bobbing up and down in the corner of the room. It was the size of a small human, it glowed creamy white and seemed to have wings. I thought it had a female form but I may have assumed this. I was fascinated but I didn't tell my sister because she was so nervous.

My mother said the next morning that her brother, Jack, who was in the next bedroom to ours, had died in the night. He had suffered from TB. My mother had nursed him for many years and later she also died from the disease. Only years later did it strike me that what I saw might have been linked to Jack's death. Did I see an angel?"

# Misty Lady
## (Clopton House, Near Stratford)

Few great houses have seen such terrible tragedies as this one. It was the home of Sir Hugh Clopton, Lord Mayor of London in 1492 and the man responsible for the handsome stone bridge over the River Avon which bears his name.

In 1564 a sweet and pretty teenage daughter of the house, Charlotte, was the first in Stratford to die of the plague and was buried in the family tomb in Holy Trinity Church. When her mother died a few days later the tomb was reopened for her, and they discovered that Charlotte had not been dead when she was buried. She had managed to break out of the coffin but not out of the vault, and had died of starvation.

About twenty years later another daughter, Margaret, drowned herself in a pond at the back of the house, it is said because she was not allowed to marry the man she loved. Shakespeare knew the family well and may have based the final scene of Romeo and Juliet on the tragedy of Charlotte, and Hamlet's Ophelia on poor Margaret. Charlotte's fate also inspired Edgar Allen Poe to write his macabre novel, *The Fall of the House of Usher*.

The Clopton ghosts are well known locally. Charlotte is said to have been seen many times in her room, while Margaret's ghost wanders round the house.

In their courting days Eileen Taylor and her husband were out one September evening when they had a most curious experience. Eileen says:

"Although it happened years ago I remember it clearly and I am sure that we did see a ghost.

We were taking the dog for a walk through the parkland around the Welcombe Hotel just as it was turning dusk. You can walk through the fields by the hotel and up past Clopton House and we were on the path at the side of the building when our little dog stopped short and his hackles

rose. Another couple were coming towards us, a young couple quite like us, who must have gone on the same walk the opposite way round. Their dog stopped too, and his hackles rose.

Then we saw a white figure at the door of Clopton House. We could only see the head, a lady's head with a cloak over it, and side view so that we could not see her face. She was not very tall and the cloak was medium grey. The top part of her seemed solid but the bottom part just dissolved into mist. She just floated across the scene and vanished into the dusk. She wouldn't have floated like that if it had been real so she was definitely a ghost of some kind, not a person. It frightened me. We met the other couple and we all said that we had seen the Clopton ghost."

The Clopton family were staunch Roman Catholics and a room on the top floor of the house had been converted into an oratory. The story is told that during the religious persecutions of the 16th and 17th centuries a priest was found there and murdered, leaving a blood stain which could never be removed, no matter how hard it was scrubbed.

The family's coat of arms includes the bloody hand, and they are not the only one. There is a common legend that such families bear this emblem because of their history. The undramatic truth is that the bloody hand is the heraldic symbol of Ulster. When baronetcies were first created in Britain they were styled 'Baronet of the Kingdom of Ulster', and they added the bloody hand to their arms as an indication of the title.

Stories of indelible stains are widely known. There is one at Littlecote House in Wiltshire and Oscar Wilde took up the idea in *The Canterville Ghost.*

# Happy Fred
## (Stratford upon Avon)

"The most haunted street in Stratford is Chapel Street and I have heard all kinds of strange stories about the buildings there. My husband and I once had an antiques shop in Chapel Street where we had some very interesting experiences.

Most of the property in Stratford is leasehold and I bought the lease of a shop which was 600 years old and had once been a public house. The building was very run down but as soon as I stepped into it I just loved the atmosphere. There were flats above which were occupied by tenants, but they moved out one by one and so we converted the first floor into one large flat for ourselves. My three children were quite small and I found it very convenient to live above the business.

As soon as I went upstairs I knew that something was there. You were aware of someone's presence, you could feel that someone was looking at you, but when you turned round there was nobody. The dog recognised it to. He was a little Jack Russell, they are sensitive dogs, and he would stand on the stairs and bark. We never actually saw anything clearly and we don't know whether it was male or female, but from the glimpses we caught it was quite small, either a young person or a child.

I think the first time that I experienced it was when something went missing. It was a very important document and I had it in my hand, but when I went to show it to my mother later that same morning I couldn't find it. I rang the people who had sent it and I'm afraid I said that I had not received it, so they posted me a copy. I felt quite guilty about that. I was very careful of this second copy and I remembered clearly where I put it, but again when I went to get the thing it was missing. This happened four times. I thought, 'Am I going round the twist or is somebody playing tricks?'.

One Saturday four members of the family and a student, who helped in the shop on Saturdays, were in the China room. We had a large cupboard into which we would put the special pieces of China, that is, those which had been reserved for customers or the most expensive pieces. Suddenly, a piece of this China came flying off the top shelf, hit the wall on the other side of the room and shattered.

A friend of ours is a computer consultant. One evening he was talking about Karate and the martial arts when suddenly he stopped talking and sat still, staring. We said, 'What's the matter?'. He answered, 'Something has just gone through the door'. We said, 'It can't have done, the door's closed.'. He replied, 'Then it has just gone through the bloody wall.'

To cut a long story short, we eventually christened it Fred. He would be around for a few days and then go missing. The thing was when he was around he would be very mischievous but everything would go right. The children were healthy, problems at school would disappear and the business would go well. We would give a big sigh of relief when he came.

My husband used to laugh at us when we said the flat was haunted, until one Sunday morning when we were late getting up because of a late night. Our little dog used to have his blanket on our bed and he would get up in the morning, go down the steps from our bedroom to the stairs door and ask to go out by rattling and scratching on the door. One morning my husband offered to see to the dog but I persuaded him that I would go, so I fed him and took him out into the garden. Then I went back upstairs with a cup of tea. We had just drunk our tea when we heard scratch, scratch, scratch. My husband remarked, 'I thought you had let the dog out'. I said, 'Yes, he's outside playing, what you can hear is Fred'. I called out, 'If that's you Fred, knock the steps', and sure enough the noise came back – 'knock, knock, knock'. After that we started to hear more strange bumps and noises. Sometimes one of my daughters would come down in the morning and complain that Fred had been in her room all night making noises.

We learned to live with Fred, in fact we grew fond of him. Some years later a friend of ours had a ghost which she called Miranda. People had seen her looking out from a window. One particular evening my daughter and I went to visit a friend and she said, 'We have had Miranda exorcised today' and she brought out some champagne to celebrate. My daughter looked at me and said, 'Miranda is still here, I can see her in the corner. Can't we take her home to Fred?'. I whispered, 'Don't spoil the celebrations and in any case, we can't start mating ghosts, we shall have little ghosts everywhere'.

Someone did some research in the archives to see if they could find out who Fred was. The only thing they discovered was a public fight where somebody had died, but I didn't think that that sounded like Fred. He was a happy ghost.

We lived there for years and years and when we moved the children wanted to take him with us. The shop is now a restaurant and when we made ourselves known to the owner recently he said, 'You know all about Fred then?'. Some bananas had gone flying across the kitchen. So we think that Fred is still there."

# Alice and the Doctor
## (Stratford upon Avon)

Almost in the centre of Stratford is a large, picturesque timber framed house which was once a coaching inn and is as old as Shakespeare's birthplace. When Felicity Bowers* and her family lived there during the 1970s part of it had been converted into a shop. She told us that many of the customers who came into the shop remarked on the strange atmosphere.

"People would say that they could feel someone else there, although they couldn't see anyone. Often we could feel something against our legs, as if the material of a dress had just brushed against us, and we could feel someone walk past.

My mother said it was Alice. She was very psychic but quite matter of fact about it and she didn't know what all the fuss was about. Mother saw Alice regularly, but I only felt her.

Alice used to open and shut doors. The middle room had two very big, heavy doors which so far as I know were original. They were awkward, so that when you opened a door you had to push it back hard to shut it. Sometimes one door would open and close by itself and then, as that door closed, the opposite door would open and close, as if someone had walked across the room.

An old lady lived next door and while we were there, her husband died. My mother went to see her and asked if she felt lonely. The old lady said that she didn't because this lovely lady in a long dress would come out of the cupboard in the evenings and sit with her. She never spoke, just sat there. The cupboard would once have been the doorway through to our part of the house. My mother's comment was, 'That would be Alice.'

We had another entity, a doctor used to come if you were ill or worried. He was just part of mum's life but I didn't see him until I was about 13. My niece was 2 years old and she and her family were emigrating to Canada. I was heartbroken, I couldn't bear her to go and I was worried about her. She was sleeping in my room, I happened to look over to her cot and bending over her was an elderly man in a frock coat, top hat, and with a Gladstone bag. He turned and looked at me with very piercing blue eyes, but there was a kindness in his expression. By his side was a boy aged 5 or 6 years wearing trousers that bulged out all round as if they were padded and a flat cap with a peak. The cap and trousers were decorated with the same pattern of diamonds. I knew instinctively that the little boy was here to look after my niece, then they both vanished. I didn't feel a bit frightened and I just fell asleep. The doctor always seemed to have a tranquillising effect on anybody he visited.

My brother always pooh poohed the idea of ghosts, but something happened on the eve of his wedding which made him change his mind. He was 21 and his bride only 19. They were both very young to get married and I know he was wondering if he had done the right thing. As he was lying in bed he felt someone sit on it, and there was the doctor with his long white beard. My brother was really terrified and said, 'Oh shit!. By the time he had put the light on, the doctor had disappeared, but my brother saw the depression on the bedclothes (made by the doctor) coming back up. After this his fear went and he was able to sleep, the doctor always calmed you.

Throughout my life I have had many strange experiences. To take one example, a few years ago I awoke one night to see the apparition of a middle aged man running across my bedroom straight at me, and he looked as if he was in quite a state. I was certainly awake because I sat up in bed and screamed. As I put the light on there was another scream, this time it was from someone in the road outside. At first I thought it was all part of the apparition but then realised that it was real. Getting out of bed I looked through the window to see a man hitting a young girl. I telephoned the police and the man was arrested and later charged with assault. Strange to say, the man who ran at me in my bedroom was not the same as the one who was attacking the girl.

I realised when I was very young that I was psychic and prone to paranormal experiences and the thought terrified me. Our house was large and rambling and upstairs was miles away from everybody. Going up there was quite scary. My brother used to make things worse by saying, 'The bogey man will come and get you.'. My mum told me to say 'God bless you.' if I ever saw anything out of the ordinary. When I was 18 I was persuaded to go along to the spiritualist church which has helped me to come to terms with my psychic awareness.

Unfortunately, the first visit that I made with the church was one of the worst experiences of my life. I went with a team of two mediums and several trainees to visit a family in Stratford who were being terrified by the apparition of an old man in long clothes and a walking stick. The whole family were living in terror in one of the downstairs rooms and using the loo down the garden. This apparition was throwing heavy furniture and leaving red handprints up the wall and over the floor. The family would scrub them out but they would reappear. There was also a black dog which left paw marks.

Our team was there to try and put the spirit to rest. We formed a circle in one of the upstairs rooms, then suddenly I felt myself moving sideways as if I had been hit and felt long sparks coming out of my legs. Falling to the floor, I hit my head and couldn't open my eyes. I knew that the old man was babbling through me but I didn't know what he was saying. I felt my body being taken down the stairs and out through the front door. My body collapsed in the street, I tried to get hold of it but it was very difficult. I felt heavy and strange and my heart was pounding.

At home afterwards I felt terrible. My mum and dad had gone to visit relatives in Canada so I was alone in the house. All my old fears of apparitions came back and I was afraid of sleeping alone. The house of the terrified family was cleared of the manifestation, but the experience affected me mentally and physically and I was left with a weak heart."

# The Man in the Trilby Hat
## (Tanworth in Arden)

"From the time we started taking an interest in the cottage to the time of the sale took nine months. The house was empty when we started negotiations but through all those nine months I was bringing bits and pieces of furniture by car. Once or twice I thought I saw something strange but I wasn't worried, the house was always comfortable to walk into; it had a nice atmosphere.

After we had been here a while and had got the house more or less straight we did some entertaining. We would be having a meal with our visitors and frequently they would say, 'Oh, somebody has gone round to your back door'. (At that time you could walk right round the cottage.) We would say, 'Oh damn, we're having a meal', and go to the back door, but no one would be there. Our visitors would say, 'We're sure we saw somebody'. We would look round the garden but we are quite isolated and there's nowhere anyone could have run to.

We would ask, 'What did it look like?', and they would describe our ghost. We saw him so frequently we gave him the name of Oscar. Oscar wore a trilby hat and a dark coat and would appear sideways as if he was going past the window. We saw most of the back of his head but no face and no hair. He used to come in any sort of weather, rain or sunshine, it didn't seem to matter.

I am a retired engineer and I try to find a logical explanation for everything. On many occasion I went into the garden to see there was something that could be related to the apparition, such as the branch of a tree, but I could never find anything.

As time went by we renovated and extended the lounge. Across the ceiling of that room was a large, black painted wooden box which was an eyesore. Late one evening I said to my wife, 'I have got to see what's under that'. We used an old fireman's axe to prize off the boarding and underneath was quite a pleasant looking oak beam which we have now restored. From that time onwards we no longer saw the man in the trilby and dark coat."

## Tricks Without Malice
### (Stratford)

"I used to live in Shipston Road, Stratford. There is said to be a Saxon burial ground at the end of the road and whether this is something to do with it or not I don't know, but at least five houses in that road were haunted. The hotel opposite to us had a lady in white who used to wander around. The guests often saw her.

The first thing I noticed when we moved to Shipston Road was when I came down one morning to find all the photographs tipped over onto their sides. That was only the start. Over and over again the doorbell would ring and I would go the door but there would be nobody there. The TV used to go on and off, often when there was no one in the room. The light outside and the light in the hall went off at the same time, and the only way for that to happen would be for someone to put the two switches off at the same time. I called our ghost, Fred, and I did wonder if he was a child because he does the sorts of thing a child would do, tricks without malice.

One evening I looked after my daughter's dog. It wouldn't settle but kept shivering and it wouldn't stay on its own. We had had the dog before and she had been quite normal. Later friends came round and we were watching TV when the box turned itself off. I switched it back on again, then when the programme had finished I switched off. It turned on again and I wondered if Fred was around.

We had a decorator working in the hall. Overnight he left his overalls downstairs and his tins in the hall. In the morning I found them in the bathroom bin. We did take paying guests but at the time only my husband and I were in the house. One guest asked if we had a presence in the house. He obviously felt Fred, but we didn't tell anyone about him because we didn't want to put people off.

One day we were crossing Clopton Bridge and the car doors were locked, then suddenly, click, click, click, and the doors were all unlocked. I said to my husband, 'Fred's in the back'.

On the last day we spent in that house I was changing all the bed linen. I had finished one bed and was smoothing out the duvet cover when suddenly, plop, from nowhere something fell into the middle of the cover. At first I thought a button must have popped off my blouse, then I realised I was wearing a jumper. Where had it come from?

Other things happened but I can't remember them all. The new occupiers have a dog. Perhaps Fred doesn't like dogs because he's gone next door. The lady there had a row of cards on a shelf and when she came down in the morning they were all turned round."

# The Clash of Metal
## (Edge Hill)

The village of Tysoe lies on the broad plain to the north of Edge Hill, scene of the Civil War battle of 1642. In our first book, *Midland Ghosts & Hauntings,* we told the story of the ghostly re-enactments of the battle which were seen shortly afterwards, and which have occurred in every century since.

In mediaeval times or earlier, Tysoe also had an ancient horse cut into the turf, the Red Horse of Tysoe, giving the area the name Vale of the Red Horse. The horse has now disappeared, presumed bolted, but there were recorded sightings in the 1940s of a ghostly white horse, thought to be Prince Rupert's charger.

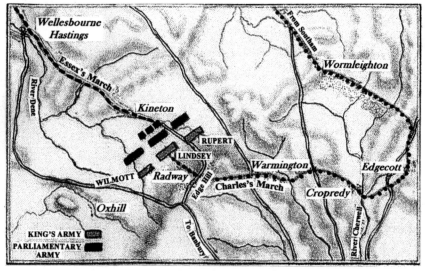

*Battle details added to the First Series Ordnance Survey map by FS Weller FRCS*

✶✶✶✶✶

"Some time in the 1970's I took my mother for a drive round the countryside between Stratford and Banbury. I can remember that it was summer time but not the exact date. We were just riding round in the car looking at the scenery and it was late evening, dark not pitch black.

We had my little dog with us, so to let him have a run we pulled into a layby near a pub. Getting out with the dog, we were surprised because he wouldn't go for a walk, he wanted to get back into the car.

We thought we could hear sheep bleating and I said to my mother, 'Somebody's frightened some sheep somewhere'. Then, I realised that it wasn't the sound of sheep, it was of men shouting. We could hear the clashing of metal and shouts like battle cries. We didn't like it. It was so eerie that we only listened for a few minutes, then got back into the car and drove away.

The next day we looked on maps to see where we had been and found it was near the place marked as the site of the Battle of Edgehill. My mother said, 'It's supposed to be haunted' so we asked around and were told about the battle. It was only then that we realized what we had heard, because I didn't know about the battle until then.

The family laughed at us and wanted to know how much we had been drinking, but we hadn't been drinking at all. We tried to make a bit of a joke about it.

I don't know whether it's coincidence or not, but from that time my mother had bad luck. People have told us that if you hear the battle you will have bad luck, and someone said that we should have gone back to listen for the battle again and that would have turned her luck round, but we never went. In any case, I didn't fancy going back. Even talking about it now it makes cold shivers go up my spine. When anybody mentions it I yelp and say 'don't mention that place'.

Unless it could be proved that it was some other noise I would say that it sounded like a lot of people in a battle. It definitely wasn't sheep, and the dog didn't like it."

# Family Ties
## (Leamington Spa)

"For several years during the 1950s my parents lived in a flat above a butcher's shop in Brunswick Street, Leamington. The building itself was part of a row of Georgian houses that had been built during the 1820's in what is now known as the 'Old Town'.

During the early 19th century a Dr Jephson discovered the healing properties of the waters and Leamington expanded rapidly in terms of houses, businesses and popularity. There were visits from royalty and celebrities such as Charles Dickens, and people came from far away to drink and bathe in the famous spa waters.

Above my parents' flat was the attic, which may have been used as a bedroom in earlier times. It had just one window which faced onto a yard at the back where an old cottage stood.

The flat had two small rooms at the front, a kitchen, a sitting room and a larger room at the back which included an old fireplace and was used as the bedroom.

During their first year my father remembers being woken up one night in the bedroom by a very cold chill in the air, although it was summer and the weather had been very warm and close. My mother remained fast asleep.

Feeling very cold and shivery, he opened his eyes and froze with fear. By the bed was a strange woman looking down at him.

Her face was an ashen white and she wore a black bonnet. Her costume was all black, long and full skirted, like that worn by women in the mid to late 1800s. She appeared to be of a middle age with a motherly air about her, and she looked down at my father with a gentle smile.

Still in shock and frightened by this sudden apparition, my father lay frozen and quickly closed his eyes for what felt like a very long time. Some time afterwards, and much to his relief, he opened his eyes again to find that she had gone.

This story fascinated me so much that it prompted me to carry out some research into the history of the house.

I found that at least three families had lived there during the 1800s. The earliest was the family of a tailor, which was followed by that of a bricklayer. Then came a butcher, Thomas Page who lived there with his family between 1881 and 1891.

Thomas Page had a wife called Elisa and four boys, William, Walter, John and Thomas, and one daughter called Flora. There were also two servants in their 20s. Tragically but not so uncommonly in those times, in 1887 Flora died at home at the age of 14, presumably from an illness.

Being the biggest room and having a fireplace, it is most likely that my parents' bedroom in the 1950s would have been used as the sitting room by those 19th century families back in the 1800s. It was in the sitting room where Flora would have lain in her coffin before the funeral, and where family and friends would have gathered to pay their respects.

Black was very much the required colour of dress for funerals and mourning dress. Even after bonnets had generally been replaced by other styles of hat, they were still being worn for funerals well into the 1880s and perhaps even later.

I discovered some coincidences of names which strongly suggest some connections between the Page family and my father.

Thomas Page was a butcher and at that same time in 1881, my father's great grandfather, also a butcher, had just opened his own shop a short distance away. Quite likely these butchers knew one another.

Thomas Page had sons called Walter and John and my father's dad was called John Walter. Elisa Page had a daughter called Flora Gertrude; my father's mother was called Gertrude.

Elisa Page would have been about 42 years old at the time of her daughter's death. Could the motherly apparition in black have been that of Elisa Page? Was she emotionally frozen in time by her daughter's death? Or was the apparition someone else who was trying to convey a message to my father?

The houses were demolished during the 1960s and replaced by a row of modern shops with flats above."

*Main photo – Brunswick Street, Leamington Spa in about 1905.*
*The house where the narrator lived over the butcher's shop is far left*
*with a canopy over the frontage. The inset photo shows the scene today.*

# Worcestershire

## Showing Her Round
### (Bromyard)

Bill Jones's grandmother was a Spanish gypsy and his grandfather a Romany, and he says that he is psychic.

"We used to have a little cottage at Bromyard. One day in May I was busy cutting the hedge when a woman appeared. She was aged about 45 and wore a yellow checked trouser suit. I started up a conversation with 'Good morning' and she said, 'You're making a good job of that'. I asked if she came from these parts and she replied, 'I was born in the cottage'. 'Never', I said, and asked her if she would like to have a look round. While I was showing her round I noticed my wife watching me with a curious expression on her face. My older daughter was not at home but my younger daughter, then aged about 3, looked amused.

I said goodbye to the woman, asking if she had far to go, and she told me that she came from Birmingham. Sometime later I said to my wife, 'I wonder what happened to that woman I showed round the cottage'. She said, 'You never showed anybody round. You were talking to yourself.'".

# Phantom Footsteps
## (Alvechurch)

Lisa Greenwood* told us that a few years ago she was friendly with a man who lived in Red Lion Street, Alvechurch.

"We used to go out occasionally and then back to his house. From the front room at different times we heard the front door open and close, then footsteps going down the passageway to the kitchen.

The first time this happened my friend said that it was his brother coming in for the night, but we found his brother already in bed. One night when we heard the front door and then the footsteps, we went to check the door, but it was still locked and bolted. Another time my friend's mother was in bed when she heard the front door and the footsteps, then they continued up the stairs and stopped on the landing. Once I was in the kitchen and heard footsteps above me in the bedroom. I thought it was my friend's brother but then he arrived home from work. There was no one else in the house. The brother said that on some nights something would come and sit on his bed, making the end of it go down.

A man who lives in the village told me that the people who lived in the house before my friend had a son who was in the army during World War II. He was killed while driving a tank, but seemed to continue going home at times when he would have been on leave. As far as I know the footsteps are still heard in the house but everyone is so used to them that they take no notice."

# Esther
## (Bromsgrove)

Sheila Armishaw was about 10 years old when all this happened and she is now 80.

"My grandmother was Jane Rogers and she lived at 34 Tybridge St. The house has now been knocked down and replaced by a petrol station. It was a very old house with some windows on the landing bricked up, something done in many houses during the early years of the 19$^{th}$ century to avoid Prime Minister William Pitt's Window Tax.

The ghost came to light when my grandmother said to my grandfather, 'The girls [my aunts and my mother] are being silly, they say the house is haunted.' He was a very down to earth retired policeman, but he said, 'That's right, I have seen the ghost twice'. Although I never saw the ghost I have five sisters who did.

We called her Esther and she used to come into a large back bedroom on the first floor. I slept in that room once and didn't see her, but I woke up crying bitterly with a tremendous feeling of sadness.

We didn't mind her at all, she was quite harmless, a middle aged woman in an old fashioned black blouse with white collar and a black skirt. She came quite regularly and would walk to the side of the bed to look down at the occupant. She seemed to be looking for someone and we thought perhaps it might be a child.

The people who lived in our house before us had two sons and they both saw her, and so did some visitors. A friend of my mother's came to stay and one morning she said, 'I know you came into my room in the night to see if we were alright, but I didn't speak to you as my daughter was asleep.' No one had gone into her room.

A vicar came and prayed in the room and afterwards my grandmother put up the picture, 'Jesus of all Nations', but it didn't stop her coming.

After grandmother died my two aunts lived on in the house until the 1970s. I sometimes wonder what became of Esther when they turned the site into a petrol station."

# Long Dark Hair
## (The Bait Box, Evesham)

Packwood's fishing tackle shop at the north end of the High Street, Evesham is called The Bait Box and it has been in the same family for four generations. The story is told by Kim whose brother is the manager.

"My brother always said it was haunted but I took no notice. Odd little things happen and sometimes the alarm goes off in the middle of the night for no reason.

One night about two years ago someone threw a stone through the shop window. The alarm rang in my house and when I got there, of course, there was a great big hole in the window. The police had turned up and they went up the stairs to interview Mick, one of the lads who lives in the flats at the back. He and another tenant had seen a car roar away and the occupants were probably the ones who had thrown the stone.

Shortly afterwards Mick asked me, 'Who was the lady with the long dark hair?', meaning someone on the scene after the stone throwing. I told him that I was the only female, and I have short, fair hair. He said, 'I saw you go out, but before you went there was another lady following the police out and she was the one with the long hair'."

# The Haunted Terrace
## (Kidderminster)

"Our house was one of a terrace near the middle of town built in the mid 1700s. A group of businessmen had pooled their money to build them and their names went into a hat. As each house was finished they drew a name and that person had the house, and this went on until everyone of the group was housed.

I lived there for only eighteen months but during that time I often had the feeling that I was being watched. We kept hearing a baby crying but there was no baby in any of the neighbouring houses. Sometimes my husband said he could hear a rustling noise like that of a long dress. My eldest daughter was two and she slept in an attic bedroom. We used to hear her chattering away but took no notice until she told us that a lady came into her room at night and woke her up.

While decorating we uncovered some early wallpaper and after that the queer events began to get worse. The dogs would act strangely, their eyes moving in unison as they watched something high up on a wall. Our decorating work had uncovered an old door at that point which had once been the top of a staircase, but the staircase had been moved.

My husband is convinced that twice someone tried to push him down the stairs. The first time he was decorating the staircase balanced on a ladder and 'it' tried to push him over the bannisters. The other time he was in the loft seeing to some bats when he felt a push down the stairs.

A lady who lived next door for six months said that she had a ghost whom she used to talk to. The ghost's name was Elizabeth and she wore a long black dress with a scarf over her head. She had died giving birth to a child that she had wanted for many years; it was a great tragedy.

A friend of a friend lived in the house two doors away and I was told that she moved out because of the strange events. She heard weird noises and had the feeling that she was being watched, but worst of all was the sensation that she wasn't welcome there. Whatever was in the house wanted her out. After I left the place I was told that there had been thirteen families in the house before us and they all had bad luck. Two people died, one fell down the stairs, one went bankrupt, another had a nervous breakdown, and so on."

# Something There
## (Hereford)

"During 2000 I moved into my Westside flat which is in an old three story building. My mother, my brother and I all think that there is something strange here.

We have seen lampshades move and heard the wind chimes ring when the windows are closed and we are certain there is no draft. Things get moved around. For example, if I leave a paintbrush out at night, the next morning it can be on the other side of the room. We have heard footsteps at 4 o'clock in the morning when everyone is in bed, then the room goes cold. We all feel that someone is there and more than once I have seen a dark, human sized shape. I saw the shape upstairs, when it seemed to be male, but I also saw it downstairs when it seemed to be different and it could have been male or female.

One day, I was putting up curtains and I heard a voice. It said, 'Go and turn the lights off and get in the shelter'. The shock of it made me hammer my thumb instead of the nail and I was so busy nursing it that I didn't think twice about the voice."

# The Haunted Cottage
## (Lickey Hills)

On the edge of the Lickey Hills is a timber framed Elizabethan cottage in the centre of a village. For a long time it was occupied by an elderly woman who mentioned several times that at night she could hear footsteps going up the stairs and across the bedroom floor.

In 1995 she moved into a wardened flat and the house was put up for sale. Perhaps it was during this time that it acquired the reputation of being haunted, because several people commented that whoever had moved in left their baby crying for long periods, when the cottage was still empty. The cottage has a shop on one side and a passage on the other. Linda lives in the village:

"There's a woman who lives in the cottage on the other side of the passage. One day she heard banging and knocking noises which went on for so long that, thinking they came from the shop, she went to investigate. She asked the man behind the counter if he could make less noise because she had a headache. He replied that he hadn't been making any noise as he had been serving customers all morning, nor had he heard any noises.

Walking back home she realized that the noises were coming from the empty cottage, at that time unoccupied for several weeks, and went right across the passage into her house

No one stayed very long in that house. A couple moved in and had radiators fitted in most of the rooms. One under the window of the front downstairs room was always cold, even when the others were hot. The repair man took it all apart to see if it was blocked, but he couldn't find anything wrong. When he put it back it still wouldn't work and no one could understand why.

The man at the shop told me that three young girls had moved into the cottage. One of them was very nervous of being there on her own and when the other two went out, she went with them. One night all three were woken up by the sound of their stereo playing loudly downstairs. They all rushed down and turned it off , then realized that it was not

93

plugged in. Soon after that they moved out. I was talking to a friend who knew a woman who was then living at the cottage. She hadn't heard any rumours about it and my friend didn't want to alarm her as she had only been there a short time. My friend asked how she was settling in and she said that the cottage was alright but for some reason she couldn't warm the front bedroom, it was always freezing cold. One night she was lying in bed in that room when she felt it go down, as if someone had sat down there, and she felt a weight on her legs. She moved out soon after.

A friend of mine started working at the shop, and at dinner time she would sit out in the back yard for some fresh air. One day she was sitting there when she heard someone washing dishes and the clinking of cups in the sink. She looked towards the source of the sounds and realized that they were coming from the cottage kitchen. No one had lived in the cottage for some weeks so she made a hasty retreat into the shop."

***** 

Many plumbing systems are under paranormal influence. The professional exorcists are called 'plumbers', and their chucking out ritual has them standing over parts of the system shaking their heads. Then they chant the incantation, 'Oh dear, dear me. Oh dear ...', then more loudly to the owner of the affected hardware, 'That'll cost you I'm afraid, oh dear me yes, that'll cost you.'. Happily the other events described in Linda's story seem like normal, straightforward ghosts.

# Happy as a Sandboy
## (Redditch)

"In the house that I used to live in before 1995 I always had a feeling that there was something strange but I was as happy as a sandboy. I loved every damn brick.

I rented two lovely rooms and before all this happened there was a young lady living in a flat upstairs. One evening when it was still light she came down and said, 'I've got a lot of flies in my bedroom'. I went up and I could hear a buzzing which I will never forget. On one side of the room was her fireplace and on the other the window, and from the fireplace to the window, all round the walls, it was thick with thousands and thousands of bluebottles, not one layer but lots on top of each other.

They covered the window and cut out the daylight making it black as hell, so she came down to stop with me for the night and her father opened the window for the flies to escape. She left the flat after that, and that's how I came to be living in the house on my own. The door to the stairs led off one of my rooms but it was always kept locked.

My son came to live with me for a short time and he told me that something had walked past him one night. I said, 'How much did you have to drink last night?'. We never said any more.

My daughter also came to live with me for a few weeks on and off. One night I was waiting for her to come back from a dance and looking at the clock when I heard footsteps overhead. Backwards and forwards they went, I go cold thinking about it. I thought that somebody has broken in because there was easy access over low roofs. Then I heard a *creak, creak* and I hoped they wouldn't come through the door. Then I heard *bang, bang, bang,* followed by *thump, thump, thump.* I was frightened. I grabbed my coat and handbag and ran to the next door neighbour. Her husband offered to get a hatchet and break down the dividing door, but I said, 'Don't do that just yet'. I rang the landlord who would not come straight away, he said he would be there in the morning.

When the landlord came we went to the flat above mine, where everything was normal. Then we opened the little door which let onto the attic stairs.

Four litre cans of paint were standing on the stairs and two dress shop models lay in pieces, arms and legs everywhere. The landlord said, 'What the bloody hell's happened here? No wonder you were scared'. There were shelves all round the attic and papers and books from them were scattered all over the floor. Some 78 rpm records looked as if they had been skimmed across the room. Nobody had broken in and it was obvious that nobody had been up there for years.

After that everything seemed to calm down but I was always wary. A couple of months later my daughter woke up in the night and thought, 'Why is mum sitting on my bed?'. As she was thinking this, she saw a woman with long, grey hair look at her and smiling. Coming into my room she saw that I was in bed.

Some months after that I was in hospital. One of my sons in law offered to decorate my living room and decided to stay overnight, but his wife went home. He woke up during the night and saw, through the glass door between the bedroom and living room, a white shimmering light. He thought, 'What's that, I haven't left the light on'. He got out of the house and ran all the way to Batchley at 6 o'clock in the morning. I had often seen this light but thought it could be reflections from the windows of a nearby factory.

One night I woke up and the light was there, absolutely brilliant. I wanted to go to the bathroom and I couldn't wait. I thought, 'If it's going to hit me, that's too bad', and I walked straight through it. When I came back it was gone. It couldn't have been a reflection from anywhere because it was pitch dark.

I often had the feeling that something was present in the flat. One evening I stood in my living room and I said, 'Whoever you are, you are welcome but please do not frighten me or my grandchildren'. I often wonder about it."

✶✶✶✶✶

Many of these events do not seem to have any ordinary explanation. Flies, though, do sometimes swarm, and we prefer to assume that they were natural.

# Strange Company
## (Crabbs Cross, Redditch)

Judy Canning's* house was newly built when she moved there in January 1985 with her 4 year old son. The other children lived with her ex husband.

"'Things' began to happen almost immediately. At first the loft hatch kept rattling and I would find it moved to one side. I was told that wind coming under the roof was moving it, but it still moved when there was no wind.

My son slept in one bedroom and I was in the other. One night I was sitting in bed when a shape emerged from the opposite wall. There was only a little light from the stairs so I could not make it out exactly, but it looked like a black net curtain coming towards me. One minute it was there and the next it had gone. Thinking it must be something to do with my son I got up to a look at him, but he was still asleep.

On evening at about 8 o'clock I was sitting in the lounge when I saw a woman's face in front of me, no other part of her, just the face. Even now it makes me feel cold to think of it. She was aged about 60, her hair was white and taken back from her face and her expression was solemn. She was quite clear, but seen as if through a net curtain. At first I thought it was my grandmother, but my grandmother was a big woman and this was a small featured person with a thin face and high cheekbones. I just sat there, staring, then I blinked and my eyes felt strange, as if there were tears in them.

From then on, through the years, we have all called the ghost 'she'. We can often hear footsteps walking up the stairs, slow but quite light, and I would say that they were those of a woman. A strange thing is that they sound as if they are on wood, although our stairs has a carpet.

When my daughter was staying here she saw the figure of a woman in her bedroom. She had wanted to come and live with me but this made her change her mind. I can understand how she feels because at first I was really frightened, but it doesn't seem to do you any harm.

I don't know whether it's the ghost or not, but all kinds of strange things happen in our house. At first I thought that I was going senile or something. I would turn the lights off when I went to bed and they would come on again, making me think I hadn't pressed the switch properly. Even my bedside lamp has been giving problems. One night I pushed at the switch but I couldn't turn it off, the button would not press. I read my book for a few more minutes and then I was able to switch the light off without any effort. We heard banging in the walls and assume it is the heating installation. I was told there was an air lock but the system has been drained and everything else possible has been done to it, yet the banging goes on.

There is no real pattern. Two or three incidents can occur in one week for several weeks then it can be quiet with nothing happening for months. Round about midday and over the Christmas period is the most likely time. Just before a recent Christmas a friend from Birmingham came to see me, someone who had been very sceptical about these tales of strange happenings. I asked him if he would like a cup of tea and he said, 'Why ask, you've already put the kettle on, I can hear it boiling'. Pointing out to him that I couldn't have done that as I had been sitting there for some time, I told him that the kettle kept switching itself on and off.

We have had many strange incidents, like when I put my duster down by the kettle and it disappeared, reappearing in the lounge. At another time I finished my ironing, put my iron down and took the clothes upstairs. My son immediately said, 'Where's my football socks?'. Only a few seconds earlier they had been there but they were gone. Later we found them in the freezer.

On top of the TV sits a clock which must not be moved or it will not work. Noticing that it had been moved to the window sill, I told my daughter off about it. She said, 'I haven't been near it, I've been in the kitchen'.

In another incident I had been collecting tokens from a national newspaper for my holidays and I kept them between the cruet pots on the table. I cleaned the table and knew where I had put the tokens, but they just weren't there. I phoned my son and asked him if he had seen them because I knew he was collecting them as well. When I went back into the kitchen the tokens were on the table just where I had left them.

One evening I was downstairs in the evening when I heard my name being called, 'Mom, mom.'. Thinking it was my son who was upstairs I shouted, 'Wait a minute, I'm coming.'. When I asked him what he wanted he said that he hadn't called me.

The ghost doesn't bother me, in fact I feel as if I have company. Since I now live on my own it prevents me from feeling lonely."

# Black Cowled Figure
## (Lodge Park, Redditch)

"These experiences happened in Lodge Park when I lived there with my parents and two brothers. Several queer things happened and I always thought there was something there.

My younger brother and I had separate beds in the same room. At the time I was about 26 and he would be 19. One night I felt something tugging at the bedclothes, pulling the sheet off my bed.

I thought that my brother was messing about. It felt as though he had tied some string to my sheet and was tugging at it. I waved my hand between the beds but there was no string and my brother was peacefully asleep. I grabbed the sheet and pulled with all my might until I had the sheet wrapped around me, then I drifted off to sleep. The next morning I wondered if it was a dream, but I saw finger marks on the sheet.

I never told my parents or my brother about it because I thought it might have frightened them, but over the years the same thing happened to me several times and I got used to having a tug of war with my bedclothes.

About a year later my brother was killed in a motoring accident and some time later I felt the floorboards in the bedroom move, as if someone was walking on them. I assumed that my brother had 'come back' and I was very nervous. I told the presence, "Please go away", and the footsteps stopped.

The sheet incidents continued but after a time they changed. I felt a pressure on my legs as if someone was sitting on my calves and feet, which was terrifying, but after a few minutes I felt the weight lift as if the person had stood up. This happened several times and eventually I said, "Will you please leave me alone.". Whenever I asked it to go, it left, and I always said "thank you and goodnight".

Some years later my older brother separated from his wife and they later divorced. For a time he stayed with my family. This meant that he and his son had to sleep with me in my bedroom, my brother sleeping in what had been my younger brother's bed and my nephew in a sleeping bag on the floor. My nephew was about 14 at that time and I did not want to add to their problems so I didn't tell them about the ghost. That night my brother felt the pressure of 'someone' sitting on his legs, and he was terrified, but because I had had the experience for so many years, I was just irritated.

One night my nephew wanted to sleep in the bed, so my brother said he would sleep on the floor. We went to sleep but later I felt someone walk into my feet, actually stubbing my toe and waking me up. I thought my nephew had wanted to go to the toilet but had gone the wrong way.

I opened my eyes and could see quite clearly by the light of a street lamp. My brother said from the floor that his son was still asleep in the bed, but glancing towards the wardrobe by the side of the window, I saw a black cowled standing figure. It did not have a face, but seemed to loom towards us and then disappeared. After this my brother and his son moved out, but neither of them ever told anyone about our experience."

# Fluke Returns
## (Stourport on Severn)

"In about 1984 I had an office in High Street, Stourport. At that time, apart from myself and my PA, Roz, only Debbie and Anne were in the building with offices along the corridor.

Strange things happened, starting with Debbie's cassette radio mysteriously changing channels and being switched off. Soon after, both women heard footsteps from derelict rooms on the top floor. What brought it to a head was when an electrician client of mine, Willy, was working late one evening to finish some work in one of the offices. Just before packing up he heard footsteps on the top floor and so, thinking he was about to lock somebody in, he went upstairs and was surprised to find it derelict with nobody there. The following day he mentioned it to me and the two women.

We were intrigued so we contacted the previous tenant to check whether they had experienced any unusual happenings. They too had heard footsteps on the wooden stairs but found no one there. Then I contacted the local newspaper, the *Kidderminster Shuttle and Stourport News*, because many years before their *Stourport News* office had been in the same building. Sensing a story they sent along a reporter who had experienced first hand a ghost when he was in the armed forces, and he picked up a cold spot in one of the offices. He took photographs of Debbie and Anne and just after that, Debbie felt something touch the back of her leg which left a red mark.

The story hit the local paper and at that point my PA, Roz, came back off holiday. She thought the whole business was a load of rubbish until the day when Debbie and Anne went into her office and said they could hear the footsteps upstairs again. One of the women was sitting down. Suddenly she was surrounded by a haze, then she shot out of her chair and the shape went up the wall and disappeared. I now had three scared ladies on my hands.

I thought what they were telling me was baloney. However I contacted the local Citizens Advice Bureau to see if they could put me in touch with someone who could sort it out. They gave me the name of James

101

Stourton* who was President of the 'British Research and Psychic Organisation'.

James agreed to come to Stourport after I agreed to pay a fee. The strange thing was he picked up the same 'cold spot' in the one office on the first floor as the man from the *Kidderminster Shuttle*. Next we went to the derelict room immediately above, where he seemed to go into a kind of trance and started to say strange things about pumping up water and repeating the name, 'Fluke'. The only explanation I could get out of him was, 'Fascinating, fascinating'. He said the name Greville was coming across to him and he thought there was a link with Warwick.

James Stourton asked us to let him know if anything else happened and suggested that we could hold a seance, however, the women were too frightened to take part.

I made some more investigations. There was a Mrs Metcalfe living off Lion Hill in Stourport who had spent a lot of time researching local history. From her we found out that our premises had once been part of an inn called the Old Bull's Head, and an old map showed that to the rear there were underground springs. There was no way that James Stourton would have known that. We also discovered that Stourport used to be called Mitton and the area had been owned by the Earl of Warwick. The Curator at Warwick Castle told me that there had been an Earl of Warwick called Fulke Greville, not Fluke. He had been murdered by his manservant but according to James this was way before our 'Fluke', whom he reckoned to be from the 18th century.

Debbie and Anne moved elsewhere and I was left on my own in the offices. For the next twelve months there were no happenings until one day when two strange things occurred. It was a wet day and about mid morning I returned to my offices from seeing a client in town. As I went through the door I was thinking I would put the kettle on for a nice cup of tea. Climbing the stairs I heard my phone ringing, so first I went into the office to answer it.

Having dealt with the call and still wearing my hat and coat, I went to the kitchen to put the kettle on. As I walked through the door I froze, something was not quite right. After a few seconds I realized what it was, the kettle was boiling, then it switched itself off. This was spooky, the hairs on the back of my neck stood up, who or what had switched on my kettle for me? I was alone in the building. I said, 'Thank you, you could have made my cup of tea as well', then I made it and returned quickly to my office.

Late that afternoon Willy, my electrician who had experienced the footsteps the year before, came to put a new brass plaque on the outside wall by my front door. Whilst he was on the pavement unscrewing the old plaque I told him about the kettle incident. By the time I had finished my story Willy was in the process of putting the four brass screws back into place to hold the new plaque. As he picked up the last screw from the shelf just inside the door, it dropped from his fingers. We both stepped back expecting it to be on the carpet, but it had disappeared.

For a few minutes we searched the porch and the pavement but couldn't see the screw anywhere. Willy said he would get another one and drop it in for me. Then he started to rewind his electrical lead but suddenly stopped. 'I can see the screw' he exclaimed, and pointed to the door frame. There inside the slot of the striking plate that the deadlock slides into, sat the screw. We looked at each other. Under the law of gravity a screw could not drop, move at right angles and nestle into an aperture on the other side of a door frame. I started laughing and said to Willy, 'It looks like Fluke is playing us up again'. Whilst Willy was still with me I phoned James Stourton to tell him of the incidents as he had asked us to keep him informed of any further incidents. He told us that 'Fluke' was just letting us know he was still around and we should consider holding a seance now that he was active again.

The seance was arranged for midnight on Saturday, 10th August 1985. Apart from myself and James Stourton, 18 people were asked to come but 7 declined.. At about 20 minutes to 12 I asked Alan, a friend of mine, to slip over the road to the Severns Club to see where Frank was because he had been keen to attend. Alan returned a few minutes later and said that Frank was acting very strangely and could not come, but would explain to me later. In the meantime Naomi Bishop from Radio Wyvern had got wind of the story from the local paper. She phoned to say that she was in the area, she would like to come and would get to us in 5 minutes.

Thirteen of us sat around in a circle as James began the séance at just after midnight. They were a mixture of work colleagues, clients and friends, Willy and his wife, Jean, Steve and Helen, Roy, Tony, Alan, Jenny, Justin and his wife Naomi, James Stourton and myself. The seance began by James saying that he was going to prepare us all into what he called a "haemolytic state" and in a sense we would all be like mediums. He went on to say that if anybody felt anything strange they were to let him know.

After about 15 minutes strange things began to happen. Steve said that he could not stop tears streaming down his cheeks, to which James assured him that it was a normal reaction. Helen said that she could feel something tightening around her neck, she was moved inside the circle and went off into a trance. By this time the room started to feel electric. Jean and Jenny both said they were experiencing a strong smell of garlic, which in Jean's case was making her feel ill. However, James told her to stay where she was and not break the circle. In my case and with Steve next to me, our heads started to go back and our jaws were moving but we both managed to break away from what was happening. Suddenly Helen and Justin started twitching, at which point James asked Roy and Tony, who had felt no effects at all, to take Justin upstairs to the second floor quickly. Shortly afterwards there was a thud, and Roy later told us that Justin had gone as stiff as a board, sat upright, then fallen back.

Hearing the thud James Stourton ran upstairs. As he did so Helen lifted her head, stared straight at Naomi and started laughing in a man's voice, then went back into her trance.

James came back down to us and switched on the lights. It was 20 minutes to 2, Helen was now okay, and James asked me where the light switches were for upstairs. I told him there was no electricity there so he asked for lighters or matches to provide light so that he could bring Justin out of his trance.

Justin came to and James said that we should get him off the premises, to which Justin turned, pointed to the corner of the room and said, `No, he wants me to stay'.

Roy said he would walk to the car with Justin and his wife but when Justin was halfway down the stairs he suddenly flew forward and stumbled down the last few stairs. I was at the top seeing them off so I asked if he was alright. He glanced at something on the stairs between him and me and stormed out. His wife drove him home. He later claimed that he had been pushed. By what? Who knows, I didn't see anything.

I went back to the others and Helen and Jenny were making cups of coffee. Both were still shaking from their experience so there was as much sugar and coffee spilt as was in the cups, so I poured the boiling water into the cups to avoid any accidents.

James reckoned that the ghost was the spirit of a person who was either hanged or strangled on the premises, although in his interview with Naomi Bishop he did not commit himself too much. Naomi summed up by saying that she was a normal, logical person but she had no logical explanation for what she experienced that evening

For a short time afterwards we had further incidents. The Monday morning after the seance I went into the kitchen to put the kettle on. As soon as I walked through the door I froze once again. This time there was a very strong smell of gas in the room, quite overpowering. I quickly closed the door and went to ask Frank and his son Bill from the nearby greengrocers if they could spare me a few minutes. I took them back to my offices and led them to the kitchen. Frank said, 'You've got a gas leak', to which I replied, 'That's what I thought at first, but there's no gas on the premises'. Bill then said that it smelt like garlic. Although the window was open the smell lingered in the kitchen for two hours

Another incident took place later after we had been given permission to use the top floor. We had a plasterer working in the end room on that floor, and when he was sweeping up he turned to see a pool of water where he had just swept. There was no explanation for it being there and when he tried to open the door to leave the room someone or something was holding the door knob to stop him. To his amazement no one else was on the premises except my new PA who was in the office on the floor below. We didn't see him again.

We had another strange incident one Saturday morning with a wrought iron clock high on my office wall. When I glanced at it to check the time I noticed that the hands hadn't moved from when I last looked. Looking closer I saw that the big hand had been bent right inwards to stop it from moving. I phoned James Stourton and told him and he said that it was being a bit mischievous.

One of the strangest incidents was when a client of mine, Bill, moved to Stourport to take over a new pub. I saw him in the High Street and invited him up to my office for a coffee. For a moment I left him in my PA's office sitting in the very chair where the lady had been enveloped by a haze. When I came back from the kitchen with the coffee I found Bill sitting very quietly, stroking his chin and acting quite strangely. I looked at him and said, jokingly, 'What's the matter Bill? You look as though you've seen our ghost'. He replied, 'You know that you've got one, then?' He said that the ghost had one of the bushiest beards he had ever seen, and that's the only sighting anyone has had.

*Fulke Greville,*
*the first Lord Brooke (1554 – 1628)*
*from a portrait by P. van Somer.*

Another strange incident that can't be explained was with an old, vivid blue poison bottle that had been found upstairs when we first moved in. I had filled it with water, full to the top, and pushed the original cork back in, then it was put as an ornament on top of a filing cabinet in the office with the cold spot. One day a new guy who had a business link with us was sitting at his desk with the bottom drawer of the filing cabinet open. He kept hearing a scraping noise every now and again but when he looked up he could see nothing. Then he heard the scraping sound again and looked up at the filing cabinet to see the blue poison bottle edge itself forward and fall into the open drawer.

I heard him call and went in to find him retrieving wet papers. Then he picked up the blue poison bottle and stood it back on the cabinet. The cork had broken off leaving a piece of cork wedged in the neck. The strange thing was that the bottle, now half empty, would not allow any water to pass the remaining cork. So how did the water get out? No matter how hard we shook the bottle not one drop came out.

The strange events continued when I again met Frank, my friend who had been eager to attend our seance but didn't turn up.

Apparently the day before and on the day of the seance a voice was warning Frank not to go. It continued into the evening of the seance when he and his wife were at the local Severns Club from where he intended to cross the road to my offices in time for midnight. When Alan went to see where he was, Frank says he was being held back by something that was not going to let him go. All evening he was in a kind of stupor which he could not explain,

However, when he got back home he suddenly became very focused and clear. That was at 1.40 am in the morning, the same time that James Stourton had switched the lights on to end the seance. Frank said that if he was offered a million pounds in a bag in my offices he would not, even to this day, venture into them.

A short time later Frank told me of another incident. He and his family were away on holiday when one night something woke him. He closed his eyes again, between sleep and consciousness, but then opened them once more to find himself in a big cellar at some time in the past. He insists that the cellar was the one below our offices when it was an inn.

On the morning of the seance I had a phone call from Stourport Library to let me know that a book I had ordered had arrived. This was *The Memoirs of Charles Cavendish Fulke Greville,* a title I had learnt from Mrs Metcalfe, the old local historian. There were a whole family of Fulke Grevilles but this Fulke lived from 1794 to 1865, so if James Stourton was correct about the ghost being of an 18th century 'Fluke', then this must be the one. It was a strange book which mentioned Malvern, Worcester and Mitton, and there was a photograph of the author's grandfather, Fulke Greville, who was bald and had a huge bushy beard." [We have added some notes about them below.]

Some aspects of this story are quite funny, like one of the Fulkes of the mighty Greville family being transformed as Fluke, or the idea of people dropping into the Citizens' Advice Bureau for help with a haunting. Still, it probably came as an interesting change from debts, neighbour disputes and County Court summonses. It reminds us of bad jokes about how, if you don't pay the exorcist's fee, your house will be repossessed.

The first Fulke Greville died in 1559 and is buried at St Nicholas's church, Alcester in Warwickshire, but the best known and most important Fulke was his grandson. Born at Beauchamp Court, Warwickshire in 1554, he was a skilled poet and playwright and represented the county in Parliament for four terms. He was Secretary for Wales for forty five years, served as Treasurer of the Navy and was Chancellor of the Exchequer from 1614 to 1622.

Fulke Greville was also ruthless, cutting down most of the oakwoods on Cannock Chase to feed his iron smelters in the teeth of national criticism and leaving the barren heath which it remains today. He was made the first Baron Brook in 1621 and endowed with Knowle Park and Warwick Castle. Greville was murdered in 1628 by a servant who thought he had been cut out of his master's will. His tomb lies in St Mary's Church, Warwick.

The author of the memoirs mentioned above was Charles Cavendish Fulke (1794-1865). Connections secured him the post of Secretary of Jamaica, a non resident sinecure. In 1821 he also became clerk to the Privy Council until 1859. Throughout his career he kept a diary later known as the *Greville Memoirs* which was published in seven volumes between 1875 and 1887. His comments on royal personages are remarkably frank and some parts of the first volumes were suppressed.

Despite the humourous elements of this tale there are one or two aspects which we think might carry a word of warning.

There are many organisations with interests in the paranormal and a desire to research it. We have never heard of a 'British Research and Psychic Organisation', athough that doesn't mean it doesn't exist. There are also many individuals who practice as diviners, dowsers, mediums, etc who will usually charge for their services, just like plumbers or decorators. Researchers, however, are usually concerned with collecting information for their own researches and do not normally charge. We put 'James Stourton's' real name to the Society for Psychical Research, Britain's oldest paranormal research organization, and they had never heard of him. They agreed with us that bona fide researchers do not normally charge for their services.

We are not at all sure what a 'haemolytic' state might be like. Our Compact Oxford Dictionary tells us that 'haem' words relate to blood, as in haemophilia, and 'lytic' to disintegration or loosening, so presumably haemolytic means loosening the blood. Perhaps this was the effect of mud on Flanders and Swann's lyrical hippopotamus.

We are also concerned about the holding of a seance to which anybody and everybody seems to have been invited, not to mention ending up with thirteen at the table which any hostess will tell you is unlucky. The seance room can generate all sorts of strange psychological effects in the sitters, apart from any paranormal manifestation, and these often release their subconscious minds.

Unless you know all the members of the group well it will be very difficult to determine what is paranormal and what is emerging from the sitters. Ill conducted seances can lead to people believing that they are possessed and suffering other psychological problems.

The Citizens' Advice Bureau may be handy and are always willing to help if they can, but we suspect that they do not have any real expertise when it comes to hauntings. You would do better to contact the Society for Psychical Research in London and asking them for a local recommendation.

By way of a postscript, when we ran this material on our word processor, the spell checker had never heard of Fulke as a name and offered us 'Fluke'. Is this a paranormal connection or merely an electronic fluke?

# Black Dog
## (The Poplars, Worcester)

"During the 1950s my family went to live in an old barn of a house called The Poplars in Henwick Road, Worcester. It was a long, flat house, three stories high, and with no front garden it looked straight onto the road. There was said to be a passage from the house to the river, and as the building belonged to the Church it was more likely to have been built as an escape route for priests than for smuggling.

My aunt had been living there but she didn't like the atmosphere, so she went back to her own home and we took over. Mother didn't like the house either. None of us liked going up into the attics, that part of the house was horrible. I especially hated one attic room but I was given the bedroom below it where I slept with my head under the bedclothes. One night I saw a ball of green light about 12 centimetres across in one of the upper corners of my room. It was just hanging there, and I felt that it was evil and horrible, not nice.

When my brother was about 18 months old he had a cot in my mother's bedroom, and morning after morning he would wake up with claw marks across his face. Not scratches from his own fingers but real claw marks. One morning he had them all over him from top to toe. We asked him where they came from but all he could say was, 'Big black dog, mum'. We did have two dogs but they were not black and they never went up there.

The house has now been pulled down and the site is occupied by new houses."

# "You will never be lonely."
## (Worcester City Centre)

Pat works in the town centre.

"In about 1986 my husband changed his job and started working in Worcester, but as we lived in Shrewsbury, we had to move house. We found a house in Worcester which we liked but the sale fell through, so my husband had to continue his daily journey. After doing it for twelve months he was getting really fed up.

However, one day he phoned me to say, 'I have found the most wonderful house'. It was in the north-western side of the city and seemed to be just what we wanted.

I had never had this feeling before, but as soon as we walked into the house I felt that something wasn't right The place was owned by an elderly couple who told us, 'We won't show you round, feel free to have a wander round by yourselves'.

Downstairs was OK. There was a family kitchen and a lovely sitting room with a nice view. I went up the staircase and was only half way up when I felt petrified. It was cold and I could almost see something on the stairs. I said to my husband, 'I don't like this house, it's haunted'.

My husband was furious and said I was being bloody stupid. I forced myself to go into the two attic rooms and had to come straight out of one of them. I could hear sounds like a high wind and I knew that there was something or someone in that room.

The elderly couple took us into the sitting room for a cup of tea. The wife said to me, 'My dear, I do hope you will buy this house, I can tell you that you will never be lonely. There is always someone here to talk to you'. I looked at my husband and he looked at me. Afterwards he said, 'That was an odd house'.

Three months went by and we still hadn't found anywhere to live, so we thought again about the house in north-west Worcester. It really was a nice house and perhaps we had been too hasty in turning it down. We decided to have another look and this time took my daughter with us. We didn't say anything to her about the hauntings but as soon as we entered my daughter said, 'This house is haunted'. She had the same experience as me.

We questioned the elderly owners about it and they said that the building had once been a school. The ghosts of the children sometimes came to visit them in the sitting room. I wasn't happy with that. If it had been just children I might have lived with them, but I was sure that there was something very strange in the attics."

# Weird Things Happen
## (Wythall)

The streets and houses of the West Midlands end abruptly at its southern boundary, and the area between Wythall and Hopwood has few roads and a scattering of dingles, heaths and farms. Some of these farms are very ancient. The dairy farm in question is listed in the Domesday Book of 1086 and is said to have once belonged to King Alfred the Cake Burner.

The two feet thick outer walls are rendered. This is a great, rambling farmhouse, with four large rooms on each of its three floors and an extension which served as servant's quarters. The line of bells which rang to summon the servants still hangs in the kitchen. In the farmyard are granaries, cowsheds, calfsheds and innumerable other buildings. The cellars run most of the way under the house and in their walls you can see the great boulders on which the house is built. The farm has been in the same family for four generations. The mother of the present owner often stayed at the farm when it was owned by her grandparents.

"My grandfather was a real Victorian. He was very strict. When I was small I had to be seen and not heard, which meant I had to sit on a seat in the window and stay there. My son now manages the farm. It's a strange place and weird things often happen. The latches rattle when there's no wind.

I was sitting in a little study next to the hall when a door slammed. The door between the lounge and the hallway is glazed, and through the glass I saw a pair of lady's legs going up the stairs.

Some workmen from Earlswood were in the farmyard with their radio on but the station kept changing. It was a push button model and they kept saying to each other, 'Have you pushed the button on the radio? When they were welding they would find that their gas bottles had been turned off. Quite a lot of lads came to work at the farm but left suddenly without coming back. One of them told us that he had seen something but he wouldn't tell us what it was.

One very windy night my son had an empty 5 gallon plastic container which he shoved behind a dustbin to stop it from blowing about in the wind. When he came out the container had moved and was sitting in the middle of the yard. The weird thing was that although strong gusts of wind were rushing through the yard and the container should have been blown from corner to corner, it was standing upright and very still.

In the corner of the yard is a long, narrow calf pen. It has a single window on one side and eight windows the other. Halfway across the long side are double doors reaching to the roof; if any light managed to get in through them it would only be a glimmer. One evening I was driving down the slip road towards the farm when I saw that lights were on in all eight of these windows. Each one of them was full of light, so it was definitely not the reflection from the car headlamps. I was surprised because I thought my son had gone to bed. I said to my husband, 'He must be working in the calf shed'. When we parked in the farmyard I saw from the side window that the lights were off. As I backed out and could again see the eight windows the lights came on again. I didn't stop to investigate, I drove off. The next day, my son said to me, 'Was it you who came in and went straight out again?' and I had to explain what had happened.

Many times, perhaps once a month, I have seen a dear old farmer in his floppy hat and a cow gown. On the first occasion I was sitting in the little study next to the front door where I saw the lady's legs when, again, the door slammed. Through the glass panel I thought I saw someone come in. A short time later I thought I heard something again and when I looked through the glass I saw this farmer. He was a greyish colour all over as if he was on black and white television.

# Photographing
# the Impossible

For fourteen years Barrie Roberts has taught Britain's first local authority evening class on the paranormal. Meeting at Great Barr GM School in Birmingham on Wednesday evenings once a month, the class is called 'Ghosts and Unsolved Mysteries'.

Among the students for some years has been Mike*, an intelligent young man always ready to argue a point of view. One evening after class he said, "I'm going to tell you a story and I know it's true because it happened to me."

He told about a neighbour who had recently moved into her house but had become so frightened by it, and one rear bedroom in particular, that she preferred to sleep downstairs. It got so bad that eventually she was sleeping in a neighbour's house.

"The neighbour knows that I am interested in the paranormal and asked me to see this woman. However, she had called the church in. so I said that I didn't want to get involved until the church had done whatever they were going to do.

Anyway, the church messed her about. First of all they said they were going to call on a certain day and didn't turn up. Then the vicar said he wasn't going to do the exorcism and was going to call in an expert. He told her that she was being haunted because she was an alcoholic and her partner was a junkie, neither of which was true". This really upset the woman, so she asked Mike to see if he could do anything.

"I decided to spend a night in the room on my own. It was just as she had said. The room became very cold, beyond reason, and I felt absolutely terrible, completely alone and miserable, with an awful feeling of rejection. I tried to think what the reason could be. I thought of all the tales I had heard. Perhaps the room was occupied by some kind of entity. I thought, in that case it needs help. I had heard that this sort of disturbance happened because 'they' couldn't get to the next world. Perhaps talking to it might help.

I felt a right Charlie sitting there in a strange bedroom talking to myself. I started talking to it and saying that I understood how it felt, but it was frightening the occupant. I started saying, 'You must move towards the light', and all of a sudden it seemed to work. The room became warmer and I felt much better. I told the woman but she still refused to sleep in the bedroom and soon afterwards moved away.

Mike produced the prints and they looked as though fresh blood had somehow become a part of the picture. However, the sheet of mini prints showed no stains and the negatives seemed faultless, suggesting that the staining had occurred in the printing rather than in photography or developing. Mike took the negatives back to Boots and, without referring to the stains, ordered another set of prints. They came back perfect, virtually proving that the first prints were accidentally spoiled by being printed on damaged or stained paper. The only other explanation would be that whatever haunted the bedroom had moved to Boots' and left a signature which, frankly, we very much doubt. We tell this story to introduce some of the problems that may occur when people try to photograph or film paranormal manifestations.

The Victorians were gadget crazy. They had table cigar lighters that brewed their own hydrogen then spouted flame through the jaws of a silver beast, railways that ran around the dining table to serve the dishes, machines to play the piano and many more bizarre devices. Photography was irresistible. Spiritualism swept into Britain from America in the mid 19th century, just as photography was catching on. In no time the serious and scientifically minded were using their cameras in attempts to photograph events in seance rooms and haunted houses, while the unscrupulous were applying every photographic trick to produce strange and puzzling images.

Accidental double exposures soon taught fakers the easy way to produce ghostly images, while hordes of skilled and dishonest mediums produced 'phenomena' for earnestly scientific photographers. They seemed easily taken in by muslin and balloons, luminous paint and cardboard cutouts. The great Sir Arthur Conan Doyle, who created the remorselessly rational Sherlock Holmes, was fooled by two teenage girls into believing that the lasses had photographed fairies by a Yorkshire brook. A respectable doctor took part in the faking of a picture of the Loch Ness Monster.

Once it became possible to reproduce photographs in the printed media examples of such fakery circulated worldwide. One famous picture appeared in a British Sunday newspaper in the 1950s. It showed a pattern of black blobs on white, which many peoples' eyes and imaginations resolved into a likeness of Christ. Half a million readers bought copies. Twenty years later it was reprinted in the same paper with the same result. This picture is usually described as rocks in the snow photographed from a plane but first appeared in Canada in 1923 as an enlarged photo of flowers in a garden.

The 1890s were the heyday of the stereoscopic camera, producing almost identical pairs of photographs which were viewed through a special viewer to give the illusion of a three dimensional scene. Stereo cameras have two lenses a short distance apart, but photographers who couldn't afford one soon learnt that a stereo pair of pictures could be created by taking one photograph, then moving the camera slightly to one side and taking another.

Difficulties arose if anything in the first picture moved before the second was taken. An object which appeared in only one of the paired photos would be seen through the stereo viewer as a transparent image adrift in a solid scene. In no time photographers capitalised on their errors and produced novelty stereo cards containing 'ghost' figures. Soon they had adapted the technique to make cards where an object appeared in different positions in each picture. Rapidly closing one eye after the other while viewing the pictures produced an illusion of movement, and the effect was applied to create comic, ghostly and even pornographic stereo cards.

Victorian cameras were cumbersome pieces of equipment using glass plates to create the negative, and another technique involved photographing an image onto a glass plate and, instead of developing it, leaving it in the camera while another picture was taken. The result would show both images superimposed and many 'ghostly' pictures were made in this fashion.

The coming of cheap snapshot cameras and roll film expanded the use of photography, but the new photographers knew nothing of the physics or chemistry of their hobby. Their films were developed and printed by the local chemist and there were fewer photos of ghosts.

116

There was one area, though, in which more ghostly images appeared. Box cameras could not handle the long exposure times needed to photograph the dim interiors of churches and public buildings so for these plate cameras were still needed. Several photographs taken with plate cameras in such places showed weird, semi-transparent figures. In every case the photographers were professionals or skilled amateurs and apparently honest. In no case had the photographer seen the figure which appeared on his plate.

One such photo was believed to be the 'Brown Lady' of Raynham in Norfolk. A picture of the sweeping staircase of the house shows a transparent female figure descending the stairs. Another was taken in the elegant drawing room of a stately home on the day that the former stately occupant was being buried. The photograph shows the solid legs of someone seated in His Lordship's favourite chair and a transparent upper body.

It was this last picture which pointed to the true explanation. Evidently the photographer, knowing that his plate need several minutes exposure in the big, dimly lit, drawing room, had opened his lens then stepped outside for a smoke. In his absence a servant had entered the room and sat in the late Lord's chair, only to realise after a moment that there was a camera on him and scamper off. The give away lies in the stockings and breeches on the 'ghost's' legs, as worn by the footmen of the house but not by His Late Lordship.

Only in the late 1970s did it emerge how often this kind of incident had led to apparent phantoms in photos taken with plate cameras. The TV programme 'Arthur C. Clarke's Mysterious World' collected a number of 'haunted church' photos and passed them for analysis to the photographic laboratory of the Metropolitan Police. All of them showed weird robed and cowled figures, some with skull like faces. By this time computer analysis of photos was available and it revealed that, while a number of photographers were standing in the porches of churches indulging their nicotine addiction, worthy ladies in overalls had entered the church, failed to spot the camera, and gone about polishing altar rails and arranging flowers. Because of their movement the images were blurry and transparent and, when their faces appeared, it was only long enough for the slow plate to record the highlights and shadows of their features.

So, are all ghost photographs fakes or mistakes? Certainly not. Sherlock Holmes said that 'once you have eliminated the impossible, whatever remains, however improbable, must be the truth'. Having eliminated obvious or provable fakes and mistakes, one is left with a hard core of photographs which seem to show the impossible. Mr Holmes might agree that these pictures must depict the truth in some shape or form.

The most frequent problem with apparent 'ghost' photos is their provenance. By the time they attract attention, not enough is known or can be discovered about the circumstances in which they were taken.

A picture was handed to Anne Bradford after one of her lectures on ghosts. It was taken at Knockin Church, Shropshire and has a date in the corner, but we didn't know if it was American style 3$^{rd}$ February 2000, or British style 2$^{nd}$ March 2000. We did not see the negative and we knew nothing about the camera's age and reliability, the skill or otherwise of the photographer, the nature of the film, the time of day or the weather, though there seemed to be sunlight through the far windows at the east end of the church.

We had a picture which seemed to show strange, star shaped things floating in the air above the pews. At lower left, one of them was actually cut by the edge of the picture. The negative would have shown whether the rest of that image appears on the film beyond the frame of the picture. If it did, then the star effect was an accident caused by faulty film or a processing error. A camera cannot imprint images on a film outside the picture frame, apart from occasional reflections which occur inside a camera pointed towards the sun. These are usually mechanical in appearance (with straight edges) totally unlike our stars.

We do not know if the photographer actually saw the stars, but we suspect not. If the picture had been an attempt to photograph them the camera would probably have been aimed more to the left, so that one star did not slip off the edge of the picture.

All in all it was a curious and intriguing picture but lack of information about it frustrated any attempt to prove the nature of the stars. Enlargement of the print showed that the shapes had very irregular edges and, forced to a conclusion, we would say that they were probably caused by cracking of the film emulsion or chemical spillage on the film or printing paper. Access to the negative would have allowed us to examine it and to get another print to see if the effect would repeat.

As it happened, a matter of days before the book was due at the printers we learnt the name of the photographer. There was not time to make the enquiries raised above and it proved impossible to agree on a fee for use of the picture, so we leave what we have written as a fair example of the sort of analysis and questions raised by ghost photographs.

By contrast we have picture No. 1 which was taken by Barrie Roberts and appeared in *Midland Sprits & Spectres*. It was taken at the home of a neighbour in Walsall who had suffered a kitchen fire. After the fire Fazal and his wife experienced various apparently paranormal effects in the house, but they also fell into dispute with the insurers. To record the fire damage Barrie went to Fazal's house with his nearly new Chinon 35mm camera, loaded with a new roll of Kodak high speed colour film.

*Photo Barrie Roberts*

*Photo 1.*
*The twisted skein of smoke at*
*Fazal's house in Walsall, taken*
*from 'Midland Spirits & Spectres'.*

The entire film was used to photograph the damage, then the film was processed and printed at a local shop. All the pictures were perfect apart from the one shown. It shows the view across the stair lobby from the rear door of the back sitting room, looking at the kitchen door. Barrie stood in the sitting room doorway with Fazal immediately behind him. Neither of them saw anything unusual as the picture was taken, there was no scent of smoke and neither of them were smoking, it was a July morning and there was no heat or fire in the house, yet a great twisted skein of what seems to be blue grey smoke appears in the picture.

The camera proved to be faultless and the film was brand new. The negative showed that the smoke effect lay within the frame of the picture and was cut off at the edges in other words, whatever had imprinted itself on the film did so through the lens as the photo was taken and it was not a film, processing or printing fault.

Now, you may think this all very negative, but the positive side is that we know that the picture is not a fake and not a technical error, but that something invisible to the eyes of two human observers was 'visible' to the camera. That information is important, and might, eventually, lead to an identification of the phenomenon.

Have a look now at the two pictures of a railway engine, No. 2. These were also taken by Barrie before a ghost watch at the Horsehay Engine Shed in Telford. You can read the story of the watch in *Midland Spirits and Spectres*, but let us stick to the pictures. The engine (which is alleged to be haunted) had been drawn into the shed where the overnight watch was to take place. The shed itself is said to be separately haunted.

At about 11 pm as the watch was about to start, Barrie entered the shed to check that all the equipment was in place and working and to take some reference photos. All the shed's electric lamps were on as he stood beside the engine and took a picture along the platform. Dissatisfied with the angle, he took a pace to the left and immediately took another shot. He saw nothing unusual at the time of either photograph, and the interval between the two exposures was only a couple of seconds. Nevertheless, one picture reveals a thick layer of what seems to be mist across the top. Had it been there in reality, it could not have dissipated in the very short interval before the second photograph was taken.

Once again, there was nothing wrong with the camera and the film revealed that the mist ends at the edges of the picture frame, so it was

*Photos 3.*
*GWR 0-4-2 pannier tank engine*
*at Horsehay Engine Shed in Telford.*

*Photos Barrie Roberts*

not a camera, film or process fault. Again, the positive result is that something invisible to a human observer has recorded itself on a photographic film at the moment of exposure. It should be added that, though the Horsehay mist is superficially similar to the smoke in Fazal's stair lobby, the coloured originals show that the Horsehay mist is white, more like steam or natural mist than the apparent smoke in the Walsall picture.

To sum up, photographic evidence can be valuable in attempting to unravel paranormal mysteries, but must be treated with great caution. There are still fakes, indeed there are studios in Europe using all the resources of computerised special effects to churn out fake spook photos and videos. There are still mistakes, accidental effects of light, odd juxtapositions of images, film faults and processing errors. Dubious photos appear in the media. A dead man's face is photographed as it appears on a family's TV screen, but a close look at the picture reveals that a key is depressed on the video recorder beneath the set, so maybe the effect is caused by a video playing. A baby smiles up at a skein of smoke alongside it, said to be the ghost of Grandma, but full versions of the photo show a small, circular dish on the floor, almost concealed by the smoke, which just might be its source. Even that experienced collector of anomalies, *Fortean Times*, published a wonderfully dramatic picture of the shadowed image of a cowled monk cast on a bank of mist by floodlights outside a church. Careful examination of the picture reveals that the shadow is that of a person wearing a hooded anorak jacket, not a cowled robe.

So keep on snapping and you may capture a ghost on film, but be careful and remember that even Conan Doyle was caught out by a pair of teenage Smart Alices.